CATCH UP

A Guide to Understanding and Using Today's Technology

By Becky Patton Logan

B's Buzz Publishing

Catch Up: A Guide for Understanding and Using Today's Technology

Becky Patton Logan

Copyeditor: Becky Johnson

Cover Design: Pam Clark

Interior Design: Becky Patton Logan

Published in the United States by B's Buzz Publishing

ISBN 9780989855501

Version 1.0

Printed by CreateSpace, a DBA of On-Demand Publishing, LL

About the Author

I can do all things through Christ who strengthens me.

Philippians 4:13

Mrs. Logan was born and raised in Olney, Maryland. She earned a Bachelor's of Education from the University of Maryland, College Park.

A serial entrepreneur Mrs. Logan's first company was Software Counseling Services which provided end-user training and support for government agencies and medium to large businesses. She later started Remember When Digital Services which provided photo and slide scanning, digital scrapbooking and video slideshow production. She was also a Desktop Support Analyst for a major law firm and wrote curriculum for the Microsoft Office suite of products for a government agency's internal training program.

She still lives in Olney with her husband, 2 children, dog and cat. The whole family fosters puppies for the Warrior Canine Connection, an organization that provides service dogs that are trained by soldiers who suffer from post-traumatic stress disorder for wounded warriors.

Contents

Preface

The Rocket Engineer and Computer Trainer Who Couldn't Turn on a PC

My father-in-law is a retired rocket engineer. He always corrects me when I call him a rocket scientist – either way, he is a smart guy. He worked for NASA for many years and helped put the satellites into space that we now use for GPS devices. He retired long before personal computers became standard and never used one at work. About 10 years ago I helped him buy his first computer and taught him some basics. It really was all he needed or wanted and never saw a reason to upgrade.

Recently my brother-in-law and his wife were visiting from out-of-town and became so frustrated with his ancient computer that they convinced him to let them buy him a new one. They selected an all-in-one, set it up for him and returned home. A few days later he called me and said he couldn't turn the d*mn thing on. I told him I would swing by and help him get started with his new PC and the updated version of Windows.

(His old PC used Windows 95 and the new one has Windows 7.)

I had seen all-in-ones in the store, but had never used one. When I found the power button, on top of the monitor, I pressed it…nothing happened. I pressed it again…nothing. I checked the power cord and surge protector which were securely plugged in and turned on. I pressed the button again…nothing. Not really knowing what else to do, I had my husband call his brother. He told us we had to hold down the power button for about 5 seconds. I pressed and held down the button and the machine booted up.

The point of the story: no one knows everything. The goal of this book is to answer the questions you feel silly asking or never even thought to ask. Have a question that is not answered in this book? Ask! See page "Let's Connect" on page 116 or send an e-mail to AskB@retiredhousewife.com.

Acknowledgements

I have truly been blown away by the amount of support I have received since I started writing these books. People like my friend Debbie Connor who makes me laugh by calling me a "badass" for writing a book. And my high school classmate, Robin Manougian who took time to tell me how impressed she was with my writing. My friend, Bart Popeck for editing my first eBook *The Retired Housewives' Overview of Technology.* Allison Willson who always encourages and supports me. My cousin Penny King for sharing my Facebook updates and designing my bee logo. My Aunt Barbara Patton for making sure I look good when I go out by keeping me dressed in CAbI. My Aunt MaryBeth Patton for never missing an opportunity to tell me how proud she is of me. All of my girls who came to the launch party for my first ebook and Valencia Lewis for making it special. My networking buddy, Becky Johnson, who offered to copy edit the book for me. Another networking friend Pam Clark who helped me design the cover. And 2 men I have never met Guy Kawasaki for writing *APE* (with Shawn Welch) and Nigel French for teaching *Design a Book* on Lynda.com And so many other friends and family members who have given me encouragement all along the way. I am truly blessed.

Dedication

I am blessed to have so many supportive people in my life. There are three in particular that have put up with a not so clean house, not so many home cooked meals and a sometimes distracted wife and mom. Thank you Matt, Sarah and Luke for your patience and encouragement, it means the world to me, because you are my world.

And a special thank you to Cadence, our foster Golden Retriever puppy, who every day at 3:30 made me step away from the computer to take her on a walk.

I'm Not a Mac Person – Don't Be a Hater

I don't understand why so many Mac people have problems with those of us who chose Windows over OS (Mac's operating system) or Android over iOS (Mac's mobile operating system). My kids tell me I am missing out on the greatest technological innovations of all times. Maybe I am, but I have never had a good reason to pay more money for hardware, learn a whole new operating system and figure out how to work a Mac's touchpad.

So, to all you die-hard Mac fans I salute your loyalty. Most of this book is written for every computer user, but there are parts that only apply to Windows users.

What You Need to Know About this Book

This book started as a print version of my eBook *The Retired Housewives' Overview of Technology*. It took on a life of it's own, but the material is based on that book, so there is some duplicated content.

This book is available both for print and for the Kindle from Amazon. There is a menu item CatchUp that has copies of all of the graphics in the book on my website www.RetiredHousewife.com/CatchUp. If you are reading this on a Kindle or using the Kindle app all of the graphics are linked to the graphics on the website.

Check the website or sign up for my e-mail newsletter for updates and revisions of this book and notifications of new releases.

Section 1: Hardware

How Do I Turn it On?

There is a huge assortment of electronics to choose from but most fall into one of the following categories:

- Desktops and Laptops
- Tablets and Hybrids
- Smartphones
- Entertainment: Televisions, Video Streaming, DVR, MP3 players
- Peripherals

Chapter 1

Desktop and Laptop Computers

In the beginning there were desktop computers, so named because they were horizontal rectangle boxes that sat on a desk, with a monitor on top. Desktops evolved into towers, which are vertical rectangle boxes that sit under the desk. As computers became crucial for doing business, the laptop came into play. In the last few years we have seen an explosion of devices on the market, with varying degrees of functionality that came into being from these two original computing devices. These include tablets, eReaders, smartphones and various combinations of all of the above. All of these devices have some basic components including:

- Processor - This is the brains of the device. It is responsible for carrying out and redirecting instructions from all of the other components.
- Memory - I can tell you what I had for dinner last night because it is stored in my short-term memory. If you ask me what I had for dinner a year ago, I would have no idea unless I had written it down in a journal that I could reference. A computer's memory holds information until it is either removed from memory or written to a long-term data storage device like a hard drive.
- Data Storage - where data is written for long-term storage. There are three types of storage: internal, external and cloud. (For more information about data storage see "Storage" on page 22.)

Other components typically found in computers and laptops include:

- Wireless - The ability to connect to the internet by receiving Wi-Fi signals;
- Graphics Card or Adapter - tells the monitor how to display data;
- Networking - Port for connecting to a network through a cable;

- Optical Drives - Drives that read CDs, DVDs and /or Blu-Ray discs (Some drives can also record to these mediums); and
- Outputs - Slots that are available on your device to connect to peripherals. These include video outputs to connect to monitors, televisions and projectors; Audio outputs to connect to speakers and microphones; Networking outputs to connect to a wired network; USB outputs to connect to a wide range of peripherals such as printers, cameras, wireless adapters and more.

Buying a Computer

When people ask me what type of computer they should buy, I always tell them put your money into the components that are most important for what you are going to use the computer for. If you have a large collection of images or video you want to store and edit on your computer, you are going to want all of the storage space that you can get. If most of your computer time is spent watching movies, put your money into a great graphics card with built-in video memory. Work with a lot of programs open at once? You want the best processor and most amount of memory your money can buy. Only use your computer to check e-mail and surf the net? Look at an all-in-one that can also be used as a television. Also think about future needs (or wants). Once you have a good idea of what you are going to use the computer for talk to a salesperson - either in person or through virtual chats. The more specific you can be, the better they will be able to help you.

Chapter 2

Tablets and Hybrids

Tablets are smaller and thinner than laptops, but larger than smartphones. As with other technological purchases, your first decision when buying a tablet is which operating system you want: Apple's OS, Android, Windows or Blackberry. Since most tablets are run on mobile operating systems, I tell my friends to buy a tablet with the same operating system as their smartphone. Many of the apps that you use on your smartphone will also be available for your tablet.

The next decision involves connectivity. If you will use your tablet mostly in range of a Wi-Fi network, either in your home, a public hotspot or a personal hotspot, it doesn't make sense to pay extra for 3G or 4G connectivity from a cell provider.

Just like a desktop computer, the processor is an indicator of the speed and power of the tablet.

With tablets, I recommend setting your budget and then buy the fastest, most powerful processor you can get for that price.

Other considerations when purchasing a tablet include the size and the responsiveness to touch. It is a good idea to try a tablet before you buy it. Make sure the size and weight are comfortable and the screen responds to your touch efficiently. You don't want a sluggish response, but you also don't want a hyper-sensitive one.

Most tablets have cameras built in, but some have two cameras - one on the front and one on the back. The front camera is used for video calls and self-photos (called selfies).

A Selfie

The tablet has spawned two other types of devices: the convertible and the eReader. The convertible is a laptop that can be converted into a tablet by disconnecting the display from the base. The biggest difference between a tablet and a convertible is the operating system. Tablets generally run on a mobile operating system where convertbles run on a desktop operating system - most likely Windows 8.

An eReader is another option. Amazon's Kindle was the first major device in this category and it is still the leader, but Barnes and Noble's Nook is a close second. A true eReader is used exclusively for reading books and documents. The Kindle Fire allows users to access the internet, stream movies and listen to music. It is actually a tablet even though it looks and feels like an eReader and is part of the Kindle family.

We own an iPad first generation, a Xoom (an Android tablet), a Kindle Fire, a Kindle PaperWhite and a Kindle. I have a docking station for the iPad with external speakers I use it as a digital photo frame and my son uses it to play music when he has friends over. I use the Xoom when I don't feel like getting out my laptop (yep I have one of those too.) I read on my Kindle Fire almost every night. My daughter has the Kindle PaperWhite, but she has not set it up so I'm thinking of taking it back from her so that I can read outside when the sun is shining (a unique feature of the Kindle PaperWhite). My husband reads his Kindle every night. We have a lot of devices, but we use them all on a regular basis.

3G or 4G?

The G stands for Generation supposedly the higher the number in front of the G the better and faster your connection to your cellular service. Be aware even if your phone is a 4G the network you are using has to be able to transmit at 4G speeds.

Another designation you will see is LTE which stands for Long Term Evolution, it's just another way to say latest and greatest.

Lesson learned, just because something sounds like a techie term doesn't mean it is.

Chapter 3

SmartPhones

All phones can make and receive phone calls. Smartphones also allow you to text, e-mail, take photos and videos and surf the internet. In fact most people use their smartphones to do everything but make phone calls. There are four options when choosing a smartphone: the iPhone, the Droid, a Windows phone or a Blackberry. They all do pretty much the same thing and whichever one you chose you will soon wonder how you every got along without it.

A Day in the Life of My Smartphone

The following is a typical day in the life of my Samsung Galaxy S3 powered by Google's Android operating system.

When I wake up, I reach for my phone and check to see if I have any notifications. Usually there are a couple of e-mails, maybe a Facebook notification and sometimes one of my apps will notify me it was updated.

As I am waiting to take my son to school, I sync my JawBone Up device with my phone and see how many steps I took the day before and how well I slept last night.

My Up by Jawbone connects to an app on my smartphone

If Luke still isn't ready, I check out Facebook and maybe UberSocial, an app I use to monitor Twitter.

After dropping Luke off, I head to the gym. Depending on what day it is and what mood I am in, I launch one of the following apps:

- Audible to listen to a book I have downloaded;
- Pandora One to listen to a radio station I have created; and/or
- Amazon MP3 Player to listen to music I have downloaded to my device.

If it is a strength training day, I launch Keep, which is a note-taking app where I have recorded my strength training routine with the weight I used during the last session. I also use the clock app to time my sets and rest periods.

After coming home and showering, I am usually in my home office. My phone is on my desk and notifies me of new e-mail, Facebook updates or Tweets sometimes before my desktop applications do.

During the afternoon, I usually run errands, checking Keep to see what I have on my running shopping list. Some days I end up waiting for Luke in a parking lot somewhere and I use the time to read either a book using the Kindle app or articles I have saved from web surfing using the Pocket app.

At the end of the day when I have settled into my chair with my Pinnacle Cherry Whipped and Diet Dr. Pepper in my 32 oz. Tervis Tumbler, I fire up the Verizon FIOS remote app and channel surf or catch up on my DVR'd shows.

Throughout the day I use my phone to text and e-mail, but I rarely use my phone to make or take phone calls.

> One morning I checked my phone to find a missed call at 12:21 a.m. from my daughter's best friend. Concerned I checked my voice mail - "Hi Mrs. Logan, it's my 21st birthday and I had to call the 21st contact in my phone and it was you. I hope I didn't wake you up." I replied at 6:30 a.m. with a text, "Happy Birthday Michelle, I hope this text notification doesn't wake you up."

Chapter 4

Entertainment

Digital Video Recorders

Digital video recorders (or DVRs) make it easy to record your favorite programs and watch them back anytime you want. To record a show you find the program using the on-screen guide or the search feature and press the record button on the remote. You will be given options to just record the episode you selected or to record the entire season. You can also indicate if you want new shows recorded or all of the shows (including repeats).

When you are ready to watch your recorded shows, you press the DVR button and all of the shows you programmed to be recorded are listed. Select the one you want to watch using the arrow keys on the remote and press Play. So much easier than programming a VCR.

Video Streaming Devices

Another option for watching television shows and movies that are not airing at the present time is a video streaming device. These little boxes connect to your television and use your Wi-Fi to stream video to your television from video streaming services like Netflix, Hulu Plus and Amazon. The devices connect to your television with video cables or an HDMI cable. After you have it connected to your television, choose Internet or Network from the Settings menu. The device will begin scanning for available Wi-Fi networks. Select yours, enter your pass code and you should be good to go. You may experience lag times as the video is buffered into the devices memory, but with a high speed connection it should only be a few minutes.

Once the device is connected, select the service you use (Netflix, Amazon, Hulu Plus, etc.) and search through the available television shows and movies until you find something you like. It can be difficult to search through the database of television shows and movies using the remote, so most services let you browse online and save shows in your "WatchList" (or something similar).

Add Duck Dynasty to Watch List with click of a button

Some of the selections may be free, some may charge a fee - it just depends on the service and your membership.

Roku a company that makes video streaming devices owns this space, with Apple TV a close second. Just today (7/25/13) Google has launched Google Cast. This $35 device connects through your TV's HDMI outlet and streams online video through your Wi-Fi connection. If you are a geek like me, or just love watching TV and movies, this is going to be a product line that you are going to want to keep your eye on.

Smart TVs

Smart TVS are televisions that act like computers. These devices integrate DVR functionality, video streaming, social networking, web browsing, apps and games into one device, the family TV set. Most TVs currently on showroom floors are SmartTVs and they will probably be one of the hot gifts this holiday season.

Chapter 5

Peripherals

Printers

The most common household printers are inkjet. These printers are cheap, easy to setup and even easier to use. The print quality ranges from good enough to near laser. Most can also print quality photos on specialized paper.

But why buy just a printer when for a little more you can buy an all-in-one that includes a copier, fax and scanner? The copier component is great for most household copying needs. The fax machine can be a little complicated to set up especially for incoming faxes, but it is nice to have if you need it. The scanner is easy to use, and useful for documents that you want to attach to e-mails. For most households it is worth the extra money to have the added convenience of these devices all in one unit.

Laser printers create much crisper text that doesn't bleed from moisture, but they are more expensive. One advantage of inkjet printers for households is the ability to print in color at a lower cost than color laser printers that are very expensive not only to purchase, but to maintain.

Inkjet printers can also be expensive to maintain. In fact when purchasing an inkjet printer you should consider how much the long-term costs of ink is going to be. I had a printer I loved, but it needed 7 different colored ink cartridges. At $12 to $20 a pop the printer was incredibly expensive to use. The last time I needed to purchase ink, I bought a new printer for the same amount it would have cost me to buy a set of ink cartridges. Like my old printer, the new one allows me to print on CDs and DVDs, but the feature that made me buy this particular printer was the built in Wi-Fi. As part of our Wi-Fi network the printer can be used by any of our devices that are connected to the network, including smartphones, tablets, laptops and my desktop.

Scanners

There are several different types of scanners. The one that is right for you depends on what, as well as how much, you need to scan. For basic scanning, an all-in-one will usually do the job. If you have a lot of documents to scan, you will probably want to get one with a document feeder. Similarly, if you have a lot photos to scan, you will probably want one with a photo feeder, and the ability to scan at a high resolution.

There are scanners that are designed specifically for scanning business cards. These scanners usually include software that extracts information from the business card and adds it to a database. There are similar scanners with software for organizing receipts.

If you have a lot of photos, slides or negatives to scan, it may be worth it to hire a service. There are many available online and the price per scan is reasonable.

Monitors

When buying a monitor the obvious considerations are the cost and the amount of space you have available. However, when it comes to monitors, the bigger the better. Many televisions can be used as monitors through a n HDMI or RGB port. If you spend a lot of time on your computer, you should really consider using dual monitors. I have my main monitor and a television that can be used as a second monitor.

My Dual Monitors

Storage

There are three types of storage: internal, external and cloud.

Internal storage is part of the device. On computers this storage is the hard drive. On other devices it is built into the hardware.

External hard drives connect through a USB port. Flash drives also known as thumb drives also connect through a USB port. Many devices have slots for memory cards. These cards are used to record images in digital cameras, record video on camcorders and/or extend storage space on smartphones and tablets. Most computers have slots for these cards. If your computer doesn't, you can purchase a card reader that connects through a USB port.

When getting rid of old electronics make sure the hard drive is completely erased or even removed from the machine and destoyed.

If you store sensitive information on a USB drive either purchase an encrypted drive (starting at around $10), password protect your files or use a third party password protection program.

More information is availalbe on my website www.RetiredHousewife.com/protect-usb-drive

Imagine all of your files floating around in a cloud available to you whenever and wherever you are. That is what cloud storage offers. When you save a file to the cloud, it is saved on a hard drive in a data center. The file is then available for you to access from any device with an internet connection. It is a great way to share files, but it is also a great way to back up some or all of your files. There are several cloud-based storage solutions available, including Dropbox, Google Drive, Microsoft's Cloud Drive and Amazon's cloud storage.

Service	Free	Price/gb	Other
DropBox	2 GB	$9.99 /100 GB	Can earn free with referrals and other promotions
Google Drive	10+ GB	$4.99 / 100 GB	Free space for Gmail storage, Google Docs, Sheets or Slides or Google+ photos larger than 2048x2048
MS SkyDrive	7 GB	$25 /50 GB	Additional 20 GB free with Office
Amazon	5 GB	$10 / 20 GB $20 / 20 GB*	*First 250 songs free, after that you can upgrade to unlimited music for an additional $10 /mo
Prices are accurate as of 9/4/2013			

Keyboards

A keyboard is a keyboard is a keyboard, right? Yes and no. Many keyboards now come with special keys and extra features. The keyboard I am using right now is ergonomically correct, has a Windows key, Windows 8 shortcut keys and has a toggle for the function keys so that they can be used for additional features like volume control and search.

Keyboards don't even have to be keyboards anymore - most devices have virtual keyboards that only appear when you need them. You use these keyboards by tapping, swyping or using the device's microphone to speak your commands and text.

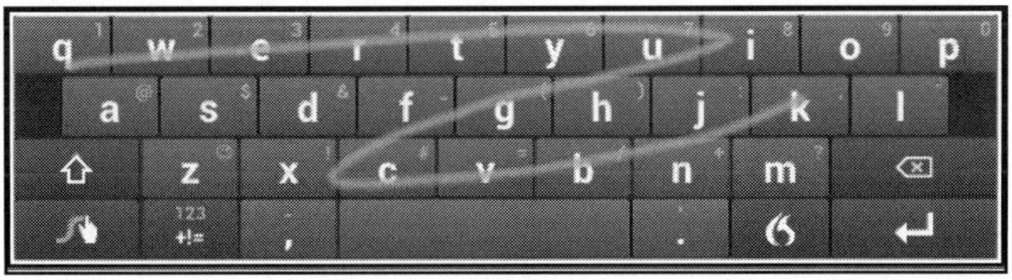

Swyping the Word Quick on a Virtual Keyboard

Mouse

The mouse is used to navigate within software. A traditional mouse has 2 buttons. The mouse performs four main actions: click, double-click, click and drag, which are all performed with the left button and right click. A single click selects an object or moves the focus of the operating system. Double-clicking selects and executes commands - it can also be used for selecting a single word. Click and drag is used to move objects - like icons and files - as well as to select text. Right click usually brings up a shortcut menu that has options relevant to the location of the mouse pointer. Scroll wheels and additional buttons have been added to the traditional mouse, which expands the functionality.

Touchpads

Laptops have always had touchpads, which are now becoming available for desktop computers. The reason for the shift is to take advantage of touch technology even when the device does not have a touch screen. Where we used to click the left mouse button to select an object, we now tap the touch pad. Double clicking is done by double tapping. Scrolling on a mouse was either done by clicking and dragging or using a scroll wheel. On a touch pad scrolling is as easy as flicking your fingers in the direction you want the mouse pointer to go.

Voice

If you have ever asked a Siri question like, "Where is the best place to hide a dead body?" you have used voice technology. Software programmers and app developers are taking advantage of the built-in microphone in most devices and are offering more voice command options.

Speakers

Sound is an important part of the digital experience. The speaker built into most devices is adequate, but you can connect to external speakers and headphones through the audio jack or wirelessly using Bluetooth technology.

> *I am regretting getting my son a good (read loud) wireless speaker for his birthday.)*

Webcams

Webcams allow you to record video which can be uploaded to services like YouTube and shared with the world. Services like Skype and Google Hangouts use your webcam to make video calls. While webcams are built in to many devices, you can also connect one through a USB port.

Networking

T1 lines and thousands of miles of cable led to thousands - probably millions - of computers being connected through an intricate series of wired connections.

Many homes connect to the internet via a router. The router receives a signal from your internet service provider and broadcasts that signal about 150 feet. Devices receive the signal either through a built in wireless receiver or a wireless adapter connected to one of their ports.

When you are away from your home Wi-fi you can connect to the internet from a hotspot or from your cellular provider. A hotspot is an area that broadcasts public Wi-Fi. Be warned that Wi-Fi signals are radio waves which means there is the potential for eavesdropping. To protect yourself be aware of what you are transmitting and on what sites. If you use a site with Https at the beginning of the URL, it is just as secure as your home Wi-Fi. Http (without the "s") sites are vulnerable to hackers.

Another option for mobile users is to purchase a hotspot. The hotspot I have is about the size of a credit card and allows me to connect up to 5 devices at a time. The device is part of my cellular package and I pay for it like

My Hotspot

it is a smartphone. The data we use through the device is subtracted from our monthly gigabyte allowance. Hotspots are great for people who travel a lot or have a vacation home and don't want to pay for internet service at two locations.

You can also access the internet through your smartphone. In this case you are using your cell provider's network to connect. Why would you prefer Wi-Fi over your cell provider's service? Typically, Wi-Fi is faster because you aren't sharing the signal with others so it is stronger.

The Story of Becky Drinks

Ever since I could drink I have been asking bartenders to make me special drinks. But I never found one that could be mine my signature drink, until one Labor Day I was at my Aunt and Uncle's home. My aunt asked my uncle to make me one of the drinks he had concocted in his "Boy's Room." The drink is simple Captain Morgan spiced rum with Cheerwine and it is delicious. We didn't have Cheerwine in our area at the time so I improvised with Diet Dr. Pepper and Grenadine. I shared the drink with my friends and called it the Uncle Keith it was the first Becky Drink.

Although I still love the Uncle Keith my current go to drink Cherry Cream Soda which is Pinnacle Cherry Whipped vodka with Diet Dr. Pepper. I have one in a 32 oz. Tervis Tumbler most nights. Although my husband points out that my "one" drink would be a triple for most.

What does drinking have to do with technology? Technology is here to stay and my generation needs to get caught up, but that doesn't mean we can't enjoy the process. It has been my experience that many things are better with a cocktail (or two), so why can't we learn technology with a glass of wine, a martini or a cocktail? I say we can.

I love trying the new flavors of vodkas, rums and other liquors. I share my favorite Becky Drinks along with technology tips, tutorials and how-tos in my books (one of which you are reading), newsletter and on my website www.RetiredHousewife.com .

So grab your alcohol of choice or even a mock tail and let's get started!

Cherry Cream Soda

* Fill a 32 oz. Tervis Tumbler with ice
* Add Pinnacle Cherry Whipped Vodka to bottom line
* Fill as much of a 12 oz can of Diet Dr. Pepper as will fit
* As you drink refill with remainder of soda

Section 2: Software

There's an App for That

Software is everything that isn't hardware. I'm not trying to be smart with that statement - it really is just the easiest way to define software. Technically, there are two types of software: the operating system and computer programs. I like to include a third category: applications. Software, programs and applications are often used interchangeably, but for the purposes of this book, I am going to use the terms specifically: software is anything that isn't hardware, programs are run locally from the computer's hard drive and applications are stored and accessed from the cloud.

Chapter 6

The Operating System : Windows

The operating system is the boss. It instructs every other part of the computer or device. The two most popular operating systems for non-mobile devices are Windows and OS. If you missed it in the introduction, I am not a Mac person (see "I'm Not a Mac Person – Don't Be a Hater" on page x). I don't have anything against Macs or people who use Macs - it is just not a product I am familiar with. For this reason, I will focus on Microsoft's operating system, Windows.

The basic design of Windows has not changed much since I taught my first Windows 3.0 class over 15 years ago. Every Windows session begins on the desktop. You can personalize the image or color of the desktop through the wallpaper settings. The desktop has icons on it that when double clicked will either launch a program or app, open a file or execute some other task.

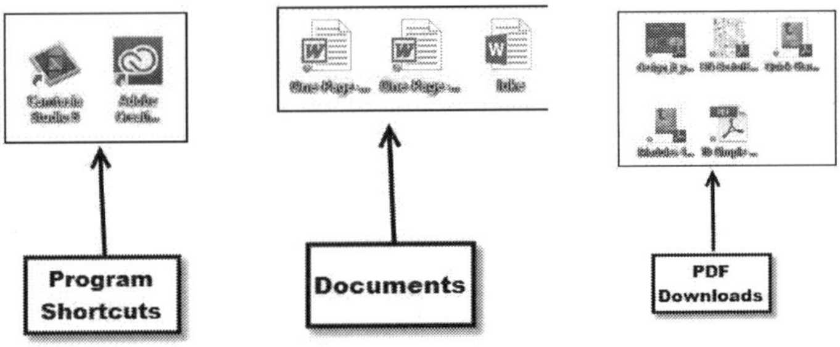

The recycle bin icon can be found on the desktop as well. When you delete a file, it is placed in the recycle bin. The default setting for the recycle bin is to permanently delete the oldest files when the recycle bin reaches 10% of your hard drive's space. Depending on how large your hard drive is, that can be a lot of files. You can manage how many files are stored in the Recycle Bin by changing the percentage. You can also manually empty the recycle bin using the Empty Recycle Bin command in the application (launch by double clicking the Recycle Bin) or by right-clicking the icon.

At the bottom of the desktop is the task bar.

(unless you have Windows 8.) In earlier versions

of Windows (before 7) there was a Quick Launch button that stored shortcuts to your favorite

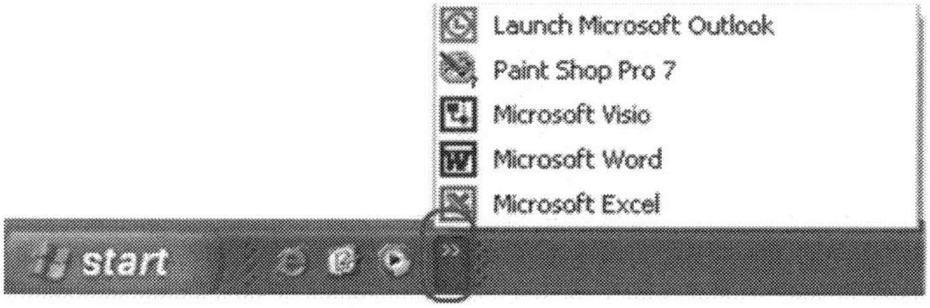

programs. Beginning with Windows 7 you can save your favorite programs right to the task bar. The task bar also shows you what applications you have open and what files within those applications are open. The system tray, located on the far right of the task bar, has a clock and icons representing system processes, like volume control and Wi-Fi connections. 

Most programs that run on Windows have a Title Bar at the top of the window. The title bar

displays the name of the application and the name of the active file. On the far right of the title bar are icons that allow you to minimize, restore or maximize, and close a window. 
Minimizing the window reduces it to an icon on the task bar. If the window is in Restore mode it can be resized and moved. When a window is

maximized, it fills the desktop. The X in the top, far right corner closes the window.

Below the title bar is the menu bar. Most, if not all, of a program's commands can be accessed

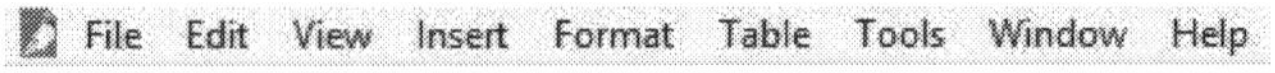

through the menu bar. When you click on a menu item, you may see keyboard shortcuts for some commands. A left-facing triangle next to an option indicates there is a sub-menu. The ellipsis (...) indicates that the command will display a dialog box, which will offer further options. This is nice to know because it means clicking on the item will not execute a command. Every dialog box has a Cancel button and a X in the upper right hand corner that will allow you to exit the dialog box.

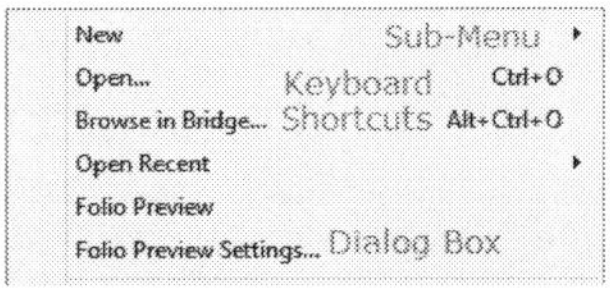

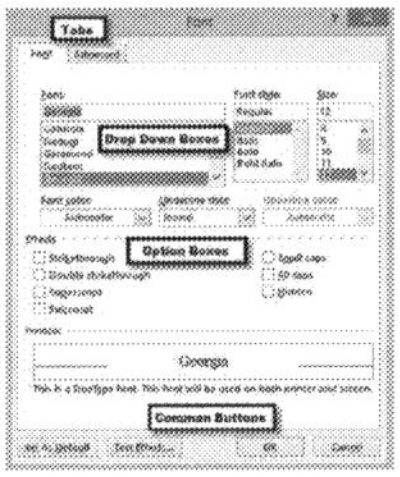

Below the menu bar, there is usually a row or two of toolbars. Toolbars feature icons that offer shortcuts to tasks and commands. Toolbars may change depending on the mode or actions being performed in the application.

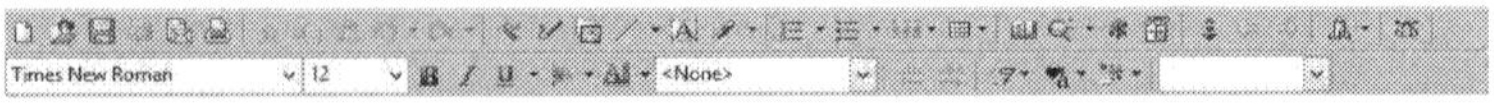

At the bottom of the window there is usually a status bar that gives you additional information

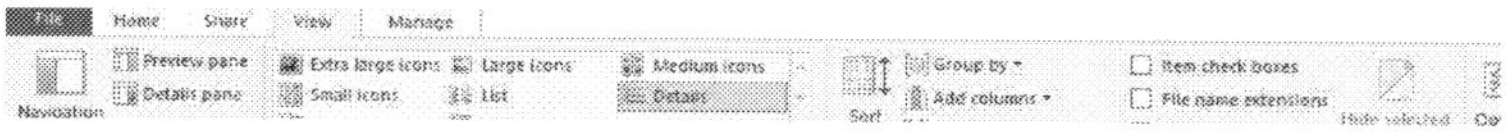

about the program, examples include what page you are on and what the current magnification setting is.

Another main function of the operating system is the organization of files. File Explorer presents files in a hierarchal structure of folders, nested folders and files. From File Explorer you can copy or move files from one folder to another, delete files and do other file management tasks.

Libraries were introduced in Windows 7. One of the Libraries already set up in Windows 7 is Pictures. This library is optimized for pictures, meaning it looks for and displays files with the image extensions like .jpeg and .png. You can add folders where you store photos from any connection including networks and external drives.

The operating system knows what program to use to open a file by the three letter extension at the end of the file name. For example, a file that ends in .doc is a Word document. If you double-click on the file from the desktop or File Explorer, Windows will launch Word and open the file simultaneously.

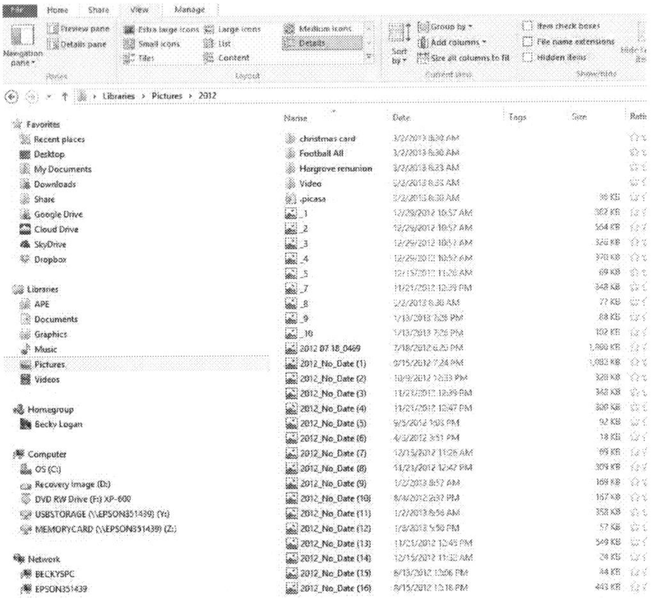

Libraries were introduced in Windows 7

Chapter 7

Types of Programs and Applications

There are literally tens of thousands - if not millions - of software programs and applications available. Most of them can be categorized either as business, graphic, lifestyle (including gaming) or utilities.

The major business programs are those included in the Microsoft Office suite which includes: a word processor; a spreadsheet program; a presentation program for creating and delivering presentations; a personal information manager, which includes an e-mail application, calendar, address book, task manager and a note-taking program; a database; a desktop publisher; and a notebook. There are other business programs and apps ranging from project management software to mileage tracking apps.

Graphic programs and apps include options to edit images, create graphics, design structures, interiors and landscapes, and create and edit video. There are also desktop publishers and applications to create projects like posters, canvases and photo books.

Lifestyle apps are available for anything and everything you are interested in.

- Like to play Scrabble? Check out Words with Friends.
- Like to watch funny video clips of cats? Check out YouTube.
- Is health and fitness your thing? There are apps that will show you new workouts and/or allow you to track your fitness regimen and progress.
- Are you a bargain shopper? Get an app to manage your coupons or rewards you for checking into stores.
- Does music speak to your soul? There are apps that will play the right song for the mood that you are in at any given moment.

- Love to read books? Then the Kindle app is a must-have for every device you own.
- Educational apps and programs are available to teach preschoolers their ABCs or help law students study for the bar.
- Love Duck Dynasty or Real Housewives? App and app.

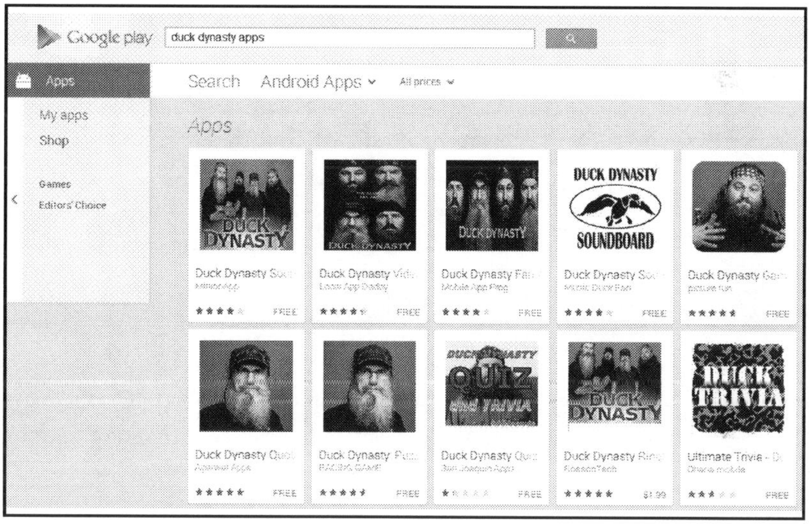

Duck Dynasty Apps

- Travel, finance, shopping and more are all available at any of the app stores: iTunes (for iDevices), Play by Google and Amazon for Android devices and the Windows app store for Windows 8 devices.

Utilities

Hackers are always looking for ways to exploit vulnerabilities in operating systems. These vulnerabilities are taken care of with another class of software called utilities. Your computer probably came with a free trial subscription for virus protection.

Virus protection programs run continuously in the background looking for threats from viruses, malware and spyware. Periodically you will need to update the index that tracks new threats to your computer. The software will usually let you know when it needs to be updated, so as soon as you receive that reminder, don't wait - do it!

You should regularly run a scan of your computer to find viruses. Even though, the program is continuously looking for threats, a new virus may make it through before the program's index has been updated with the virus' inoculation's instructions.

Utility programs also help you keeep your computer running fast, with programs to perform routine maintenance tasks. One such task is to clean out your cache. Cache is where the operating system holds files that are in use. Files can get left in the cache when you turn your computer off without going through the recommended shutdown process. When the cache is too full, you will lose functionality and your system will be sluggish.

Another maintenance task is defragmenting. I once had a job as an Administrative Assistant and one of my duties was to file documents into folders and put them in the correct drawer of a filing cabinet. That is what defragmenting does for your hard drive. It finds pieces of files, rejoins them and puts them back where they belong. This process makes it easier for the operating system to find the complete file, making it faster to access and deliver to you. Every 6 months or so you should see if your disks need to be defragmented. Windows comes with a disk defragmenter program.

Also included in the utility family are programs that backup your data. I use an online backup service, but, honestly, when the subscription runs out, I probably will not renew it. All of my important files are stored in the cloud, so they are always backed up. The cloud doesn't have features like version control where I can restore a previous saved version of a file, but I have only used that feature one time in the last 3 years, so that is not a deal breaker for me.

Chapter 8

Learning New Programs and Apps

This chapter was largely influenced by *Computer Literacy for Windows* taught by Garrick Chow on Lynda.com.

Whenever I am faced with learning a new program or application, the first thing I do is explore – take a look around to see what is there. I hover my mouse over icons to see what pops up; I click through the menus looking for what options arc availablc. I might create a new file and see what templates are there that will help get me started. If a Start-up Wizard is available I use it. I know there will be a learning curve soI try to figure out if learning the new program or application will be worth my time. Learning a new program or application is just like learning anything else - start with what you know and then go from there.

There are at least 5 things that are common to almost every program, whether for a Mac or PC. First, there is almost always a File menu. From this menu, you can Create a new document (spreadsheet, presentation, or something else), Close the window, Save and Print. In Windows, you will find the Exit command in the File menu. For Macs, the Quit command is usually located under the program name. *Note: If you only have one file open in an application Close will shut down the application.*

Second, cut, copy and paste commands are available. The cut and copy commands take whatever is selected (text, an image, etc.) and places it on the clipboard. The clipboard is a program included with the operating system that holds items that are being cut or copied. The paste command retrieves the item from the clipboard and places it in the active document at the insertion point. Because the clipboard is part of the operating system, you can cut or copy something from any program and paste it into any other program. Even after an item has been pasted, it is still available on the clipboard until something else is placed on the clipboard (in its place) or the computer has been shut down.

Third, the undo command (keyboard shortcut CTRL+Z) does just what its name implies: it undoes your last action. In some programs, you can continue using the undo command to undo several actions sequentially. Some programs also have a Redo command which undoes the undo. These are useful commands in a variety of situations, but I especially like using them when I am editing a photo and want to see if I like a filter or effect better than another one. I can quickly compare different versions using the undo and redo commands.

Fourth, preferences or options are a set of commands that let you customize the program or application to your liking. For example, if you prefer inches to centimeters on the ruler or want files saved in a specific location, find the Preferences or Options dialog box. You may have to look around for this command. Some programs place it on the File menu, others on the Tools menu. I've even seen it on the Edit menu.

Fifth, there is always a Help menu. You don't have to memorize commands. If you need a feature or want to know how to do something, search the Help file.

A great way to look for useful commands pertaining to a particular task is to right-click in an area of the screen where the task would be completed. For instance, if text is selected, right click with your mouse placed on the selected text, you will probably get common options like the ability to change the font type, size and style or to cut or copy the selected text.

If I don't get an answer to my question from the Help files, I go to the internet and type my question in the search box of my favorite search engine. Usually there are thousands of results to choose from. Other resources available to you are tech support, forums, social networks and me. You can send your technical questions to me by e-mail to AskB@RetiredHousewife.com, post your question on my Facebook page www.Facebook.com/RetiredHousewife or Tweet your question to @BeckyPLogan. I am happy to answer any and all that I can. And remember, there is no such thing as a stupid question!

Sangria

There are some great options for serving a crowd, but one of my favorites is Sangria. Traditional Sangria is made with red wine, brandy, sugar and club soda with cut fruit marinated in the mixture. But a quick search on Pinterest will show you hundreds of options for Sangria. This is my favorite (so far):

* 1 bottle Arbor Mist Sangria
* 1 cup Pinnacle Tropical Fruit vodka
* 1 1/2 cups Orange Juice
* 1 cup Pom Pomegrante Juice
* 16 oz. Ginger Ale
* Pomegranate seeds and sliced fruit

Mix all ingredients together and let blend overnight in refrigerator. If you want to marinate the fruit put it in a seperate container so it doesn't soak up all the liquid.

Section 3: Everyday Technology

Help! It's Everywhere

Pretty much everything we do involves some type of technology. We scan our own groceries, get money out of a machine, and get directions from a pleasant voice emitted from our car's radio. Our photos are digital and instead of being stored in shoe boxes or drawers, they are on memory cards and hard drives. We are entertained with various types of boxes that display books and stream video. We communicate with friends and family via e-mail, text, and status updates. You may be like me and think all of this stuff is cool or you may hate it - either way technology is all around, so you might as well learn to make the most of it.

Chapter 9

Photos are Now Images

In some ways the more things change the more they stay the same. Even though our photos are now digital, they still need to be sorted and organized. There are some great free tools available for this job. Most photo organization tools allow you to tag faces, and some even have a facial recognition feature, which tags people in images for you. These apps also allow you to attach geographical information, descriptions, keywords and categories to your images.

Most photo organization apps and programs also have basic editing capabilities including:

- Crop - simply means to cut out the unwanted parts.
- Rotate - allows you to rotate the image in any direction.

- Exposure - allows you to adjust the brightness and contrast.
- Colors - allows you to control the saturation and the temperature of the colors.
- Sharpen - helps define the edges of the image, but it cannot make a badly focused image clear.
- Resize - this is useful if you are going to share the image online.

Most apps and software programs go further than simple editing and give you fun effects and tools to enhance your images. These include special filters, stickers, doodles and text.

Editing Options in most photo editing applications

Some of my favorite editing apps are Picasa, available in Google+ and PicMonkey. If you need more advanced features, PhotoShop Elements is a good choice.

Sharing Images

You have several options for sharing images, including social media sites, online albums and digital frames. You can print images from your home printer. If you would rather have them printed professionally, you can take your memory card to a DIY kiosk, which can be found in almost any big box store. Many of these stores also let you submit your images online for printing and will have them waiting for you when you get to the store.

There are apps available on the internet for creating photo books, posters, photo canvases, iPhone covers, t-shirts and more. My favorite site for creating photo projects is Heritage Makers. In the interest of full disclosure, I am a Heritage Makers consultant, which means that if you go to my site, www.RememberWhenDS.com, and make a purchase, I will earn a commission. To learn more about Heritage Makers, send me an e-mail to Info@RetiredHousewife.com.

Here is a 12x12 digital scrapbook page I did of our foster dog Ruby.

12x12 Digital Scrapbook page using Heritage Makers

Resolution and File Types

Understanding Resolution

In Physics and Chemistry the term resolution means "the act or process of separating or reducing something into its parts." When applying this definition to digital images, whether scanned or taken with a digital camera, resolution refers to the number of pixels (parts) per inch. Pixels are squares which hold one piece of color information. If there are enough pixels per inch (200 ppi), the human eye does not see the squares, it sees one continuous image (the picture).

The resolution of the image is important if the image is going to be printed - particularly if it is going to be printed at a large size. For instance, I have a great image of my son playing lacrosse. To print well (pixels will not be visible to the naked eye) the image should be at least 150 ppi, so the biggest image of my son playing lacrosse should be printed at is 12x10:

1800/150=12

1500/150=10

Digital Image

It stands to reason that the more pixels an image contains the better. However, there is a price to be paid for all those pixels: file size. The larger the file, the more room it takes up on storage devices. If you share your images online, large images upload and download slower than smaller or compressed images. It is easy to compress your images - just save them in a file format that offers compression.

File Formats

The most common file format is the JPEG or .jpg. JPEG stands for the Joint Photographic Experts Group. This file type offers a lossy compression, which means it discards information it considers to be irrelevant. You can control how much compression takes place weighing the size of the file against the degradation of the original. Every time you open and save a JPG file, it is degraded a little more. With all the pixels in most images the degradation is not noticeable, but you still want to be aware of this and, if possible, save all of your original images to another device and work with copies.

A .png file is a Portable Network Graphic file. PNG files use loseless compression which is kind of like those space airbags. You put your clothes in the bag, suck the air out with a vacuum cleaner. The bag and clothes are compressed so they take up much less space. When you open the bag and let the air back in, the clothes and the bag return to their original shape and size. PNG files also allow you to preserve transparent areas of an image, which is important in some design projects.

PSD stands for PhotoShop Document and is used to save images that are being edited in PhotoShop. When working in PhotoShop, it is common to create layers for different elements. If you think of a traditional scrapbook page, the background paper is a layer, the frame around the photo is a layer and the photo is another layer. To maintain these layers the image must be saved as a psd file. t is a good idea to save the file in psd format in case you need to make changes to one of the layers. But in order to share it or use it in most applications you will have to save it as a .jpeg or .png. To do that you will need to flatten it.

Chapter 10

Media is Now Digital

Music

There are a variety of ways to listen to digital music, but they all start with the audio file. The most common audio file format is an MP3, which is why dedicated audio players are called MP3 devices.

Computers, tablets and smartphones can be used to play digital music in a variety of ways. One way is by storing the music on the device and using an application like iTunes, Windows Media Player or Amazon Cloud Player to listen it. Another way is by streaming music through applications like Pandora, Spotify or iHeartRadio. These applications are easy to use - just download one from an app store and follow the setup instructions. If you run into problems use the Help file or do a Google search or send me your question (see "Let's Connect" on page 116).

Podcasts

Podcasts are like live or recorded audio programs. They can range in length from one minute to over 100 minutes. The easiest way to find, download and listen to Podcasts is through iTunes. There are podcasts for every topic from parenting to technology. One of my favorites is Grammar Girl. These podcasts are usually less than 10 minutes long and they explain grammar in a way that is easy to understand. You can find podcasts to listen to or follow in iTunes or through an application like Stitcher.

Video

Many cable and satellite providers offer television shows and movies through an OnDemand service. Through this service you can rent or buy a movie with just a few presses of your remote control.

Services like Netflix, Hulu Plus and Amazon offer video streaming of thousands of titles. Not just movies, but complete TV series, exercise videos and documentaries delivered right to your smart TV, video streaming device, computer, tablet or smartphone. Most of these services are offered through memberships with monthly subscription fees.

Television

Have you ever wondered what your friends were watching? Have you ever wanted to talk about a show you love with other people who love it as much as you do? Applications like GetGlue and Zeebox allow you to do both of those activities virtually. On GetGlue, you can collect virtual stickers when you do certain activities like watch the season finale of The Batchelorette. When you have collected 20 virtual stickers in 30 days, you can request the real stickers be mailed to you. Come on - who doesn't love stickers?

Zeebox is attempting to reinvent the way we watch television. The app allows you to chat with others watching the same show in a virtual TV room. While you are watching the show, tags pop up that are directly related to what is happening on the screen. From these tags, you can get more information about people and topics that are being mentioned on the show. I hate it when I am watching a show and can't figure out where I recognize an actor from. With Zeebox I can easily figure out what shows or movies I have seen them in before. The people who launched this app call it Veg 2.0. If you decide to check it out, follow me at Becky Patton Logan.

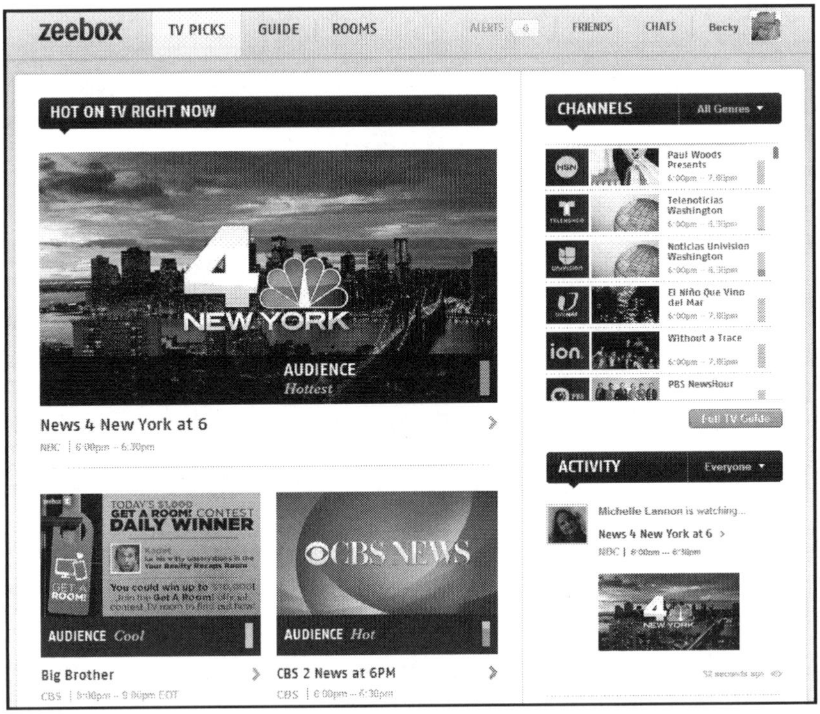

Screenshot of Zeebox website

Zeebox can also help you find something to watch. The home page features programs that are hot or populat at that very moment.

Chapter 11

Communications

E-mail Programs

E-mail programs allow you to send and receive e-mail messages. They have options to Reply to the sender, Reply to All the recipients and/or Forward the e-mail to someone else. Most programs also have the options of cc and bcc. Cc stands for carbon copy, a leftover term from the days when we made copies by typing a letter or memo on 2 sheets of paper with a piece of carbon paper in between. Bcc stands for blind carbon copy. None of the recipients will see the bcc recipients. For your peace of mind, know that if you Reply to All in response to an e-mail with bcc recipients, the bcc recipients will not receive your reply.

Most home users and even small businesses have cloud-based e-mail. Some common providers of cloud-based e-mail are Yahoo, Gmail, and just recently Microsoft Outlook. These providers offer a web-based app for managing your e-mail. You can set up local based e-mail programs like Outlook to send and receive e-mail from these cloud-based accounts. If you choose this option your mail and other personal data are stored on your computer's hard drive.

Another common feature of e-mail programs is an address book, which is a database of your contacts and their personal information. With this feature, you only need to type someone's name in the Name field of a message and their e-mail address is retrieved from the address book.

Spam

The widespread use of e-mail has created a huge spamming industry. Spam is the equivalent of junk mail. Most e-mail providers have spam filters in place which do a pretty good job of catching spam before it reaches your inbox. The problem is that sometimes the spam filter misidentifies an e-mail that you do not consider spam and puts in the spam folder.

It is a good idea to regularly check your spam folder to see if an e-mail you wanted to see ended up in the folder by mistake. If this happens, use the Not Spam button 

on the toolbar to let the filter know not to mark e-mails from this sender as spam.

Conversely, if you are getting e-mail in your inbox that you consider spam, use the Spam button on the toolbar to let the filter know to put e-mails from that sender into the spam folder.

Spam Options in Yahoo Mail

Hackers and Passwords

Hackers want your e-mail password so that they can use your account to spam all of your contacts. Make your password hard to hack, but easy to remember, by creating an acronym for a phrase. For instance, I listen to the song *Done* by The Band Perry almost every day while I am working out. So I took the chorus line, "All I want to be is DONE," and created the password AIw2biD*NE. This password is difficult to hack, but easy for me to remember. It is a good idea to use both upper and lower case letters, numbers and symbols.

Experts recommend changing your password every 90 days. I change mine on the first day of each new season.

Another way to minimize the damage a hacker can do is to have different passwords for different applications. I know you are thinking, yeah right, I can barely remember one. How am I ever going to remember several different passwords and which one I used for which application? One suggestion is to use the same password but add a letter to identify the application. In the example above, I may use the same password for Facebook but put an F at the beginning, FAIw2biD*NE. You can also use the password feature on your browser or install an add-in (extension in Chrome) like LastPass that stores all your login information in a password-protected database. (Just don't forget the password.)

Phishing Scams

A phishing sceme is an e-mail that is smeant to look like it is sent by a reputable company, but in fact it is an attempt to get personal information or plant malware onto your computer.

If a company asks for personal information or you suspect phishing don't reply or open any attachments. Report the phishing scheme to your e-mail provider and /or send to the company being imitated. Most have an e-mail address phishing@nameofcompany.com.

If your not sure where to send it go to the company's website and search for phishing in the Help menu.

Managing E-Mail

It is a good idea to have at least two e-mail addresses - one for your friends and family and one for everyone else. Whenever you have someone odd, like the grocery store clerk ask you for your e-mail address, give them the second one. Also, use the second address for online forms such as when you sign up for an e-mail newsletter. The exception to this rule would be when you sign up to receive my newsletter, Tipsy Tech Tips at www.RetiredHousewife.com.

You can have both addresses come to the same inbox. To differentiate the two use filters or rules to direct e-mail sent to a specific address to a folder. Filters and rules help keep your inbox clutter free and organized. You can usually find the dialog box for setting up filters and rules under Settings or Tools. If you have problems finding it or are confused about your options, use the Help menu or send me an e-mail to AskB@RetriedHousewife.com.

Texting

Texting has been included in cellular phone plans for a long time, even flip phones have the ability to send and receive texts. I have an application, MightyText, installed on my phone with an extension in my desktop browser that allows me to send text messages through my phone from my computer. Their most recent release integrates text messaging with Gmail.

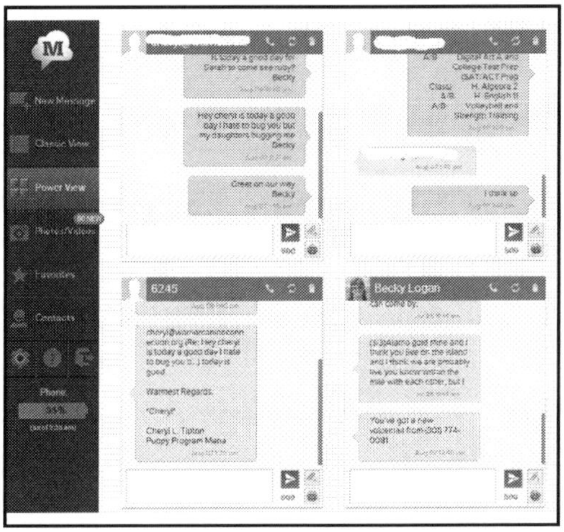

Screenshot of MightText

I have another app on my phone called Messenger that lets me text anyone who I am friends with on Facebook, as well as people in my address book.

Chatting

Chatting is the ability to have real time conversations with people who are online. These conversations can be instant messages that are written and replied to or face-to-face through video. Chatting is available through Facebook, Skype, Google Hangouts and other services.

If you are already on Facebook, the sidebar displays a list of your friends who are available to chat. Just click the name of the person you want to chat with, type your message and hit send. If the person is not available, the message will be delivered to their direct message box.

To use video chat in Facebook, you need to install the Facebook video chat plug-in. You do that by selecting one of your friends who is online to start a chat with. In the chat box click the camcorder icon. You will be prompted to download the plug-in. Once it is downloaded, click the file to launch setup and that's it - you are ready to start video chatting.

To start a chat or video call, go to the person's profile and click the call button. Note: this button will only be available if the person is online and available for chat. If they don't answer you can leave a video message.

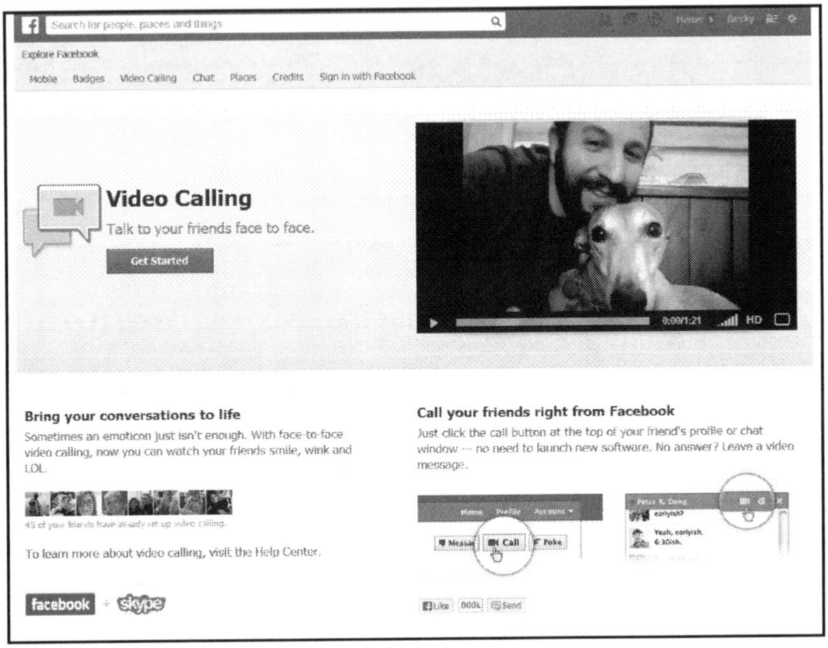

Not on Facebook? Will never be on Facebook? You can still video chat either through Google Hangouts or Skype. For more information on these services see their respective Help sections. I try to be available for video chatting a few hours every week day. If you need someone to practice with, give me a call or send me a text to 240-257-2899.

Chapter 12

In The Car

When my kids were little, I used to play a guessing game with them. On trips that they were familiar with, I would ask each one to guess the exact time we would reach our destination. Now, the GPS calculates our arrival time based on how fast we are going, how many miles we have left to travel and what the speed limit is for those remaining miles. Some GPS programs even take current traffic conditions into consideration when calculating arrival time.

When using a GPS navigator, make sure that you have the correct state or region selected. I have become frustrated with "the stupid thing" not finding an address only to realize that I had not switched the GPS to the proper state or region.

Many newer cars offer Bluetooth technology. This technology allows you to talk on the phone hands-free through your car's stereo system. Some systems will even read text messages to you and allow you to reply using only your voice. This is one of those things that you might not think is a big deal until you have tried it. Then you will wonder how you ever got a long without it.

Once you're connected to your stereo system either through Bluetooth or a USB port (some cars have them), you can use other apps on your smartphone. You can listen to your music collection, your Pandora stations or an audio book you have downloaded.

All of this technology is relatively easy to set up. If your car has these features there will be a screen with buttons. Press the menu button, and then go through the options. You may be surprised at what is available and how easy it is to set up.

Don't be afraid to push the buttons!

Bloody Mary

There is only one thing this Maryland girl likes better than vodka, crabs with lots of Old Bay seasoning mix. My Bloody Mary combines the best of both.

- Moisten the rim of a glass (or Red Solo cup) with water and dip in Old Bay seasoning
- Fill 1/3 of the glass with vodka (I prefer pepper
- Fill remaining 2/3 with Zing Zang Bloody Mary mix

Set-up a Bloody Mary fixins' bar with:

- Horse Radish
- Worcestershire sauce
- Celery salt
- Extra Old Bay
- Choula (or other) Hot Suace
- Pickled green beans
- Celery
- Bacon

Tip: I like to marinate grape tomatoes in pepper vodka to use a garnish. Make sure to break the skin so the vodka can get inside.

Section 4: The Internet

From the World Wide Web to Web 2.0

Media comes from the word medium, which, as anyone who watches Long Island Medium knows, is a conduit of information from one source to another. Traditional media is one sided, you can scream at your television all you want but no one but the people you live with will hear you. You may be able to get an op-ed published in a newspaper, but that could take days or weeks. Radio is probably the most social of traditional media, but callers still go through a screening process. In the early days, the Internet was a source of information and it offered some limited interaction in forums and chat rooms, but it was mostly used as a resource and was filled with static text.

The ability to comment on blog posts began the transition to social media, which is also known as Web 2.0. Readers of a blog post could offer immediate feedback, to which the author could respond in a virtual conversation. The conversation moved on to other social sites, including networking sites like Facebook, bookmarking sites like Pinterest, news sites like Digg, photo and video sharing sites like Instagram and YouTube and wikis like Wikipedia.

Chapter 13

The Browser

The evolution of the web can be seen in the evolution of web browsers. A web browser is software that allows you to access the Internet. Some say it is an operating system for the cloud. Most of us started on the World Wide Web paying for a service like AOL or Prodigy. Those service providers supplied every component of Internet service: access, browser, e-mail and to generate advertising revenue they tried to keep their customers on their family of sites.

As the web grew, and more options were offered, users began purchasing or getting free of charge the different components from different providers. Today the only component we pay for is access, usually through the same company that provides our other communications and media services (i.e. the cable company).

Microsoft led this shift by integrating their web browser, Internet Explorer, into Windows 95 as a value-added service. Apple quickly followed suit with its web browser, Safari. Mozilla's Firefox grew out of Netscape, which had been a for-pay service like AOL. Google Chrome was last to the dance in 2008, but as the leading search engine, they have quickly gained market share.

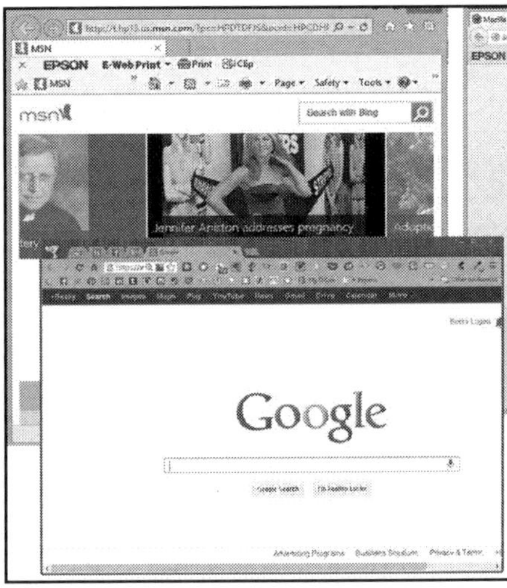

Top Left - Internet Explorer
Top Right - Firefox
Bottom - Chrome

Any vehicle can get you from point A to point B, but some are smoother, faster and more enjoyable to ride in than others. It is the same with web browsers. Each will take you where you want to go, but they offer different experiences. Just like you can add features like Bluetooth and XM radio to a vehicle, you can add features to a browser.

These features are called extensions in Chrome and add-ons in Internet Explorer and Firefox.

The Browser Window

Continuing with the vehicle analogy, all vehicles have certain characteristics like an engine, steering wheel, brakes and tires. Likewise, browsers have common features.

The Address Bar is the text box where you type in the address of the website you want to visit. It begins www, but you usually don't have to type the www. You can also use the address bar as a search tool by typing in your query. Your default search engine will return a list of sites that match the query.

Tabs allow you to have more than one website open at a time. Usually I have Gmail, my calendar Facebook and Goole+ open. I use a feature in Chrome to pin these tabs so there is more space to see other tabs that I have open at the same time.

Add-ons (in IE and Firefox) or extensions (in Chrome) are applications that run inside your browser to help you do common tasks faster. These applications provide extra features and functionality to the browser. If all of these features were built into the browser, it would become bloated with many features that you may never use. For instance, one of the extensions I have installed and use often is Pin It. The Pin It button lets me pin images that I find from websites onto one of my Pinterest boards. Pinterest's Help section has detailed instructions for installing the Pin It button in every browser, just search for "pin it button."

Favorites are shortcuts to websites that you visit frequently. The next time you are on www.RetiredHousewife.com, click on the star in the address bar, select where you want to add the favorite and click OK or Done. The star will turn yellow indicating the site is a favorite. You can go ahead and do that right now - I'll wait. Thanks.

Your browser keeps track of sites you have visited (unless you go Incognito in Chrome or In-

Private Browsing in Internet Explorer). This can be useful to not only see what sites your husband or kids have been visiting, but also to help you find a site that you have visited but can't remember what the web address is or how you got there. The keyboard shortcut to view the browser's history is CTRL+H.

The browser keeps track of files (documents, images, programs) that you download. The keyboard shortcut for the download log is CTRL+J. You can also find your downloads in the download folder through File Explorer. Unless you have moved them or changed the default download folder.

Cleaning Your Browser

I find it hard to concentrate when my office and desk are messy and cluttered. The browser does many of the same types of tasks, I do in my office, keeping track of open websites, logging activity and finding information. So it just makes sense that it responds to commands much faster with regular cleaning.

Every so often I will take a good look at the items I have pinned, taped and magnetized around my desk and office and get rid of things that are no longer useful or inspirational to me. When I do this I feel like I am able to more quickly focus on the things that I need. In the same way, when you clean out your browser's history, it is better able to predict future queries, because data from three months ago is no longer part of the educated guess.

We discussed cleaning out the operating system's cache in Chapter 8. Your browser also has a cache that needs to be cleaned regularly. In fact, if you have problems with a website loading properly or if downloading things becomes really slow, you should clean out your cache. Every browser is a little different, so use your browser's Help file or do an Internet search to find out how to clean your browser's cache (or e-mail me at AskB@RetiredHousewife.com)

I have certain things in certain places on and in my desk. I have black pens in a wine glass, colored markers in a bee coffee cup, and Post-It notes in my desk drawer. I like having these things in these places because I know every morning when I come into my office that they are going to be right where I left them. Websites remember how you left their site by leaving little pieces of code on your computer called cookies. Some people worry about this exchange of data from your computer's browser to web servers, but I like it. When I get to certain websites, I know my settings are going to be the same as the last time I was at that site, just like I know when I grab a pen from my wine glass it will be black. That said, I do occasionally clean out my cookies. But, before I do, I try to go through and save the cookies from sites I use the most (like Amazon). Even so, I know that for the next few days, even weeks after I clean out my cookies, I will probably have to reconfigure some of the sites I visit.

Troubleshooting Browser Problems

Whenever you have problems with your browser - it is running slow, something won't download or open - the first thing you should do is run a virus, spyware and/or malware scan (see "" on page 43).

Second, clean out your cache, your history and your cookies.

Third, see if the problem occurs in a different browser - if you use Internet Explorer try Chrome, if you use Chrome try Internet Explorer.

Fourth, close everything down and reboot the computer.

Fifth, do an Internet search using the keywords of the problem.

Sixth, if the problem is site specific e-mail the site's webmaster or tech support.

If all of that fails have an expert look at.

Chapter 15

The Search Engine

The amount of data available on the Internet is almost uncountable. In fact, there is a movement to create a new term, "hella," which would be a prefix for a number with 27 zeros after the first digit in order to be able to properly measure the amount of data available. All of that data would be useless if there was no way to retrieve information in a reasonable amount of time. Search engines give us this ability.

Data that is accessible by the Internet is stored on computers all over the world. Search engines send out pieces of code, called bots or spiders, to read, categorize, rank and organize data into indexes. In order to provide the best results to a user's query, search engines use an algorithm based on over 200 criteria, including data on keywords, location and popularity of the website. The exact algorithms are guarded secrets and change often.

There are two types of search results: organic and paid. The organic results are based entirely on

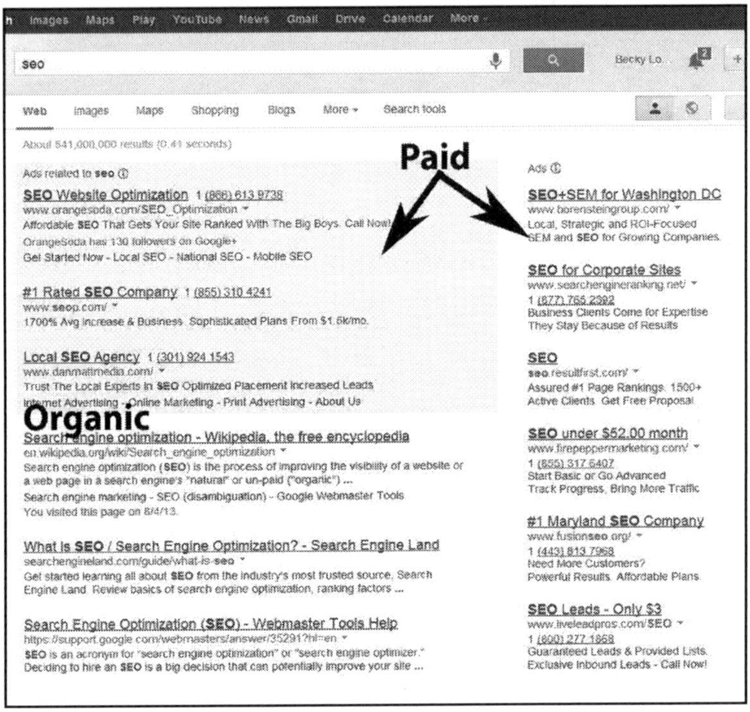

the search engine's algorithm and the owner of the search engine (Google, Microsoft, Yahoo, etc.) is not paid a dime to display them. There is an entire industry dedicated to help websites rank higher on search engines through search engine optimization. Why? Because the higher a site ranks, the more likely users will be to visit it and generate income for the publisher either through direct sales, affiliate marketing or ad revenue.

Search engines rely on publishers and advertisers. A publisher is anyone who shares information on the Internet - from multi-million dollar companies all the way down to and including me, a retired housewife from suburbia. Advertisers are anyone who wants to buy advertising space on search results pages, in applications and/or on websites. Ad networks created by search engine companies bring these two groups together.

Using Google as an example, to advertise on Google's extensive network, businesses enroll in their AdWords program. Advertisers use AdWords to create ad campaigns around keywords. When a user searches for the keyword, all of the advertisers who have campaigns for the word enter into an auction. The winner of the auction has their ad displayed - either as a paid search result or on a website or application that allows Google to serve ads on their site. You need more than the highest bid to win an auction. The exact algorithm is guarded but the same criteria used to determine organic results is used to determine paid results with the added criteria being the amount the advertiser is willing to pay to win the auction.

Advertisers can either pay an amount per click (cost per click or CPC) or per impression (cost per impression or CPM). With cost per click campaigns, advertisers only have to pay if a user actually clicks on the ad. With cost per impression campaigns, advertisers pay for every 1,000 impressions.

Ranking high in search results is big business sellers and publishers take advantage of search engine optimization (SEO) and search engine marketing (SEM). Search engine optimization attempts to gain ranking by using the right keywords in the right places and promoting the site for backlinks (other sites linking to the site).

Search engine marketing attempts to win auctions for ranking in paid results and on websites and in applications. The same tactics are used as in search engine optimization, but ad campaigns are created and a dollar value is placed on keywords. Highly searched words and phrases in competitive industries are the most expensive. In fact one click on the phrase "New Orleans mesothelioma lawyer" was at one time worth as much as $370.53. The phrase commanded so much money because it was highly competitive as well as highly profitable.

Chapter 16

Blogging

Back in the days when the Internet was just beginning to be widely available, some techies began using it to share their lives, mostly with friends and family in online journals called web logs. The term web logs was later shortened to just blogs. Being techies, they looked for ways to help make creating these blogs easier and with more features to enhance the reader's experience. As it became easier, more people began blogging. Many blogs were started by Moms of young children as a way to share funny stories and accomplishments with family and friends. Because blogs were interactive, women were able to, and did, comment on each other's posts and share experiences and advice.

This network of Mommy bloggers found out just how powerful they were in 2008 when Motrin created a short video about baby slings. The premise of the commercial was that baby slings were great accessories and may even be beneficial for baby bonding, but they caused backaches. Oops! Mommy bloggers were - let's just say - mad. They took to their blogs and to the emerging microblogging site, Twitter, to express their outrage. One enterprising Mommy blogger created a nine-minute video showing happy Moms with their babies in slings interspersed with screen shots of angry tweets. Motrin posted the commercial on a Friday and pulled it Sunday morning. The event was significant because companies started to realize how important this group of women were. Not only did they have a platform that could ruin a million dollar ad campaign, they had buying power and influence over other women with buying power. Mommy bloggers changed word of mouth marketing forever.

Blogging is no longer just for techies and Moms. Everyone from big business and government agencies to cats and dogs have blogs. There is a blog for every topic you can think of and there is room for more. If you are thinking of starting a blog, there are four questions you need to ask yourself.

> ## Four Questions
>
> 1. Do you want to make money directly from your blog?
>
> 2. Are you going to use your blog to promote a product or service you are already selling?
>
> 3. What is your blog going to be about?
>
> 4. What blogging platform are you going to use?

First, do you want to make money directly from your blog? If not, pick a platform and get started. If you do, you have several options. You can allow an ad network like Google's AdSense to serve ads relevant to the topics you write about. When readers click on the ads served on your site you will be paid per click. The amount depends on a lot of different factors including the amount of traffic your blog receives.

Another potential revenue stream is affiliate marketing. When you become an affiliate for a product or service, the seller pays you a commission on any sales made from affiliate links on your website. Amazon offers one of the best and easiest to use affiliate marketing programs available. Other affiliate networks are available and easy to find with a Google search of "affiliate networks."

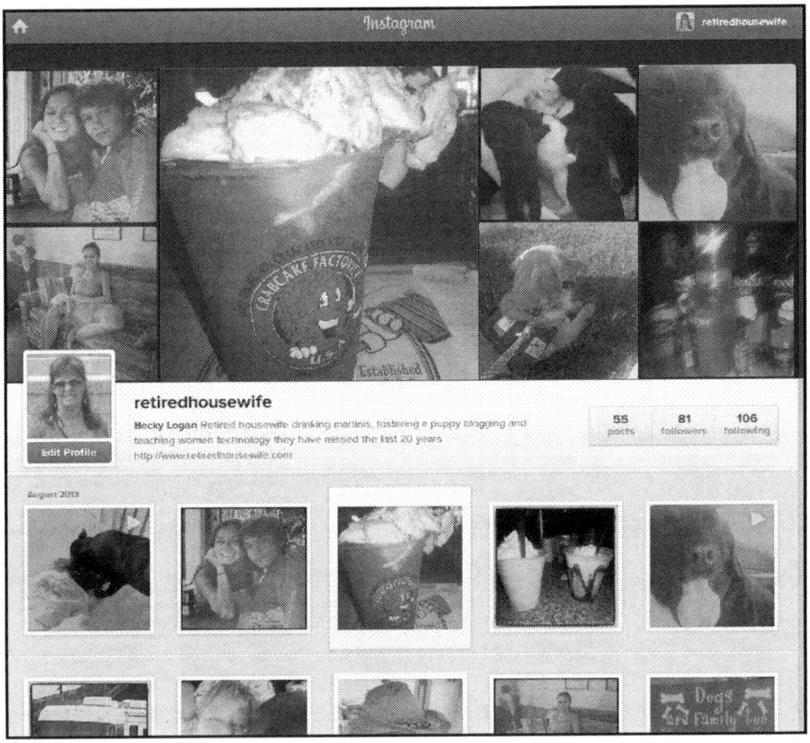

When you have established your blog and you have a steady flow of traffic, you can solicit sponsors, either on your own or through a network like the SITS Girls (www.thesitsgirls.com).

Second question is, are you going to use your blog to promote a product or service you are already selling? If so you want to be careful about setting up an ad network on your site. It is not worth the money you will make per click if a reader of your blog clicks on your competitor's ad and leaves your site to go to theirs.

Third, what is your blog going to be about? Be specific. I started my blog thinking I was going to write about everything and anything that is important to middle-aged women. I became overwhelmed with all the possible topics and ended up writing a blog post about shape-wear, followed by one about using technology. There was no focus, which not only confused readers, but made it difficult for me to decide what to write about. Now I write about everyday technology and share cocktail recipes for women my age (45-60) who are starting the next chapter in their lives after raising kids. This is specific enough, but also provides me with a wide range of topics to write about.

Fourth, what blogging platform are you going to use? A blogging platform is the software you use to create your blog. The easiest platforms are

Tumblr and Blogger. Deciding between these two depends on the type of content you intend to share. If most of your posts are going to be written, Blogger is a good choice. If your posts are going to be visual (photos, video) or short text, Tumblr is a better option. WordPress.com is also an option if you are not planning on offering ads from an ad network on your blog.

Blogging Platforms

Blogger

Tumblr

WordPress.org

WordPress.com

With any of these platforms, you won't have to worry about hosting your blog. It will live on the servers of the company offering the service. One of the advantages of Blogger is that it is owned by Google. If you want your blog to be found by users of Google's search engine, having it hosted on Google's servers' gives you an advantage.

Yahoo recently purchased Tumblr and, so far, there have been no major changes. Tumblr has a unique culture - lots of good information mixed in with some craziness (some may say inappropriateness). If you are thinking of eventually taking your blog to the next level, WordPress.com is a good choice because the next level will probably be WordPress.org.

WordPress.org is an application that is self-hosted. In the past, that may have meant having a server in your house, but now it means you pay a company to host the files that make up your blog. If you go the self-hosting route from the beginning, you will need to register a domain name like RetiredHousewife.com. It is easiest to use the hosting services of the same company. GoDaddy and HostGator are two companies that offer both domain name registration and hosting services.

Chapter 17

Social Media

To many people the term social media means social networks, specifically Facebook. But the term actually describes 5 types of websites: social bookmarking, social news, social networks, social photo and video sharing and wikis.

Social Bookmarking

Social bookmarking sites are used to save, organize and share documents, photos and videos found on the web. Pinterest is a good example of a social bookmarking site. As I surf the web, I may find something that I want to save, like a cocktail recipe for a martini. I use the Pin It button (an extension for my browser, see "The Browser" on page 85) to pin it to my Martinis, Mojitos and Other Cocktails board on Pinterest. The next time I am looking for an interesting martini to make, I can easily find the one I pinned on my martini board.

One of my Cocktail Pinterest One of my Boards

As of today, I have 232 people following me on Pinterest. One of these followers may see the pin and think that they might like to make the martini one day, so they repin it to one of their boards. If I tag my pin with a word like vodka, my pin will show up in a search on Pinterest for vodka. If the searcher likes my pin, they may look at the board I pinned it to and decide to follow my board. It is the virtual interaction of sharing information that makes social bookmarking different than just adding a website to your browser's favorites.

Social News

Social news sites allow users to submit stories that they find interesting. Some sites are moderated with the administrators deciding which the order the stories will be ranked. Others allow users to vote, which is how the story's ranking is determined. The most popular social news sites include Reddit, and Digg.

Social Networks

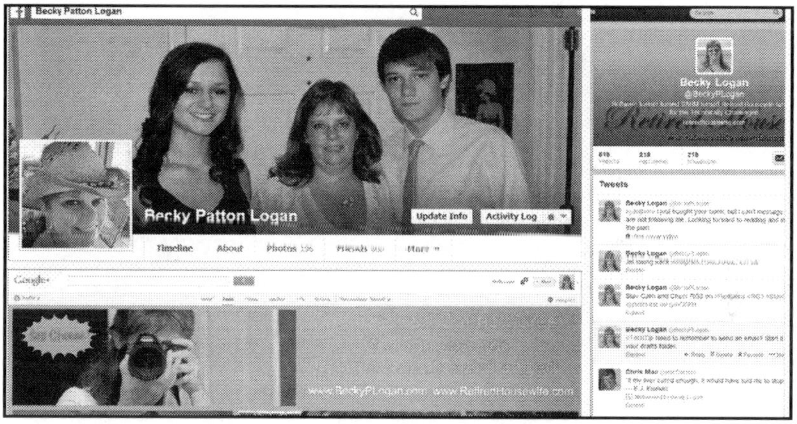

My Facebook, Twitter and Google+ Profiles

Social networks are like virtual parties or events. Facebook is what your wedding day would be if you could invite everyone you and your intended had ever met. Twitter is like a three- ring circus with so much going on it is impossible to catch everything, but it is fun to watch and even more fun to participate in. LinkedIn is a business networking event where everyone is talking about what they do and even bragging a little. Google+ is like a conference or convention where you meet people who have the same interests and passions as you. All of these sites allow you to share your thoughts, photos and videos with friends, followers or connections. Most of the conversations take place in public on your wall, but you can use direct messengering to privately share information.

Social Photo and Video Sharing

The most well-known of the social photo and video sharing sites is YouTube. YouTube has thousands if not millions of videos on every topic you can imagine.

A new player to video sharing is Vine. Vine is an application that allows you to shoot a non-consecutive six-second video. Not surprising given it's time restriction Vine is owned by Twitter.

Instagram, which is one of the most popular photo sharing sites, has recently added the ability to shot a continuous 15-second video. The appeal of Instagram is the ability to edit and add filters to photos and videos. I like Instagram because I can share a photo on Instagram and also have it post to Facebook, Twitter and Tumblr.

As with all the social media sites, social photo and video sharing sites allow users to follow each other and like and comment on posts.

Wikis

A wiki is a website that collects content from users and allows other users to edit and add to the original content. The best known wiki is Wikipedia. This massive collection of collective knowledge is available for anyone to use and/or contribute to. The most infamous wiki is WikiLeaks, which publishes original source material regardless of classification. While wikis are the largest group of collective knowledge they are not considered a credible source for the same reason that they are the largest group of collective knowledge: anyone can write whatever they want on wikis. Many of the sites are moderated and edited, but there are still a lot of inaccuracies. They are good sources to find answers to simple questions like definitions of terms and well-documented knowledge.

Dessert Drink

I'm not much of a milk drinker so when I ran across cocktail recipes with half and half I wasn't interested. Still I kept coming back to ne and decided to give it a try and I am glad I did.

2 parts Pinnacle Chocolate Whipped vodka
* 1 part Godiva White Chocolate Liqueur
* 2 parts half and half

Rim the martini glass with chocolate syrup and multi-colored sprinkles

Wrap-Up

Some 20 years ago I taught a group of senior citizens Windows 3.1. Many of them were tentative. But one woman jumped right in. She was asking me questions faster than I could answer them. She loved everything about the computer. At the end of the class she thanked me and apologized for asking so many questions and then she said something that melted my heart.

"I wish I had been born 40 years later so all this cool stuff would be at the beginning not the end of my life."

She was 85 years old so if she had been born 40 years later she would have been in her mid-40s. I remember thinking at the time she should have wished for 60 years earlier, but now I know the 40s are the perfect time to learn new things.

For me my children are more independent and I'm not spending nights and weekends at practices, games, helping with homework or one of the million other things I loved doing with my children when they were younger. I know what I like to do and maybe more importantly what I don't. I certainly do not care about what people think of me, if I ask a stupid question on Twitter, so what? If I have typos or grammatical errors on a Facebook post, oh well. If my kids think I'm unhip because I don't use Apple products, no problem.

Learning new technology does not have to be a frustrating, hair pulling process. It also doesn't have to take place in a classroom on a week night when you have a million other things you would rather be doing. It can happen anytime, anywhere, just use your device, check my blog regularly for tips, tutorials and how-tos and continue to purchase **The Retired Housewife's Guides for the Technically Challenged.** If you run into problems or have questions I'm an e-mail away.

Let's Connect

I regularly blog at www.RetiredHousewife.com, post tips on my Facebook page and share useful information on Twitter. I am working on my YouTube channel which will feature how-to videos. I share more of my personal life on Instagram with photos of cocktails, my family and pets. From any of these social media networks you will find out when new eBooks and books are published.

If you have enjoyed this book, please write a review on Amazon.com or GoodReads.com

You can ask me questions at Questions@RetiredHousewife.com

If you would like me to speak at an event please send an e-mail to Becky@RetiredHousewife.com

Social Networks

Blog	www.RetiredHousewife.com
Tumblr	www.BlogByB.com
Facebook	www.Facebook.com/RetiredHousewife
Twitter	@BeckyPLogan
Pinterest	www.Pinterest.com/beckyplogan
Instagram	RetiredHousewife
Google+	Becky Logan
LinkedIn	www.linkedin.com/in/beckypattonlogan
YouTube	Becky Logan
GetGlue	@becky_patton_logan
Zeebox	Becky Patton Logan
Skype	beckyplogan@outlook.com
GoodReads	RetiredHousewife

Keyboard and Mouse Shortcuts

Windows System

- F1: Help
- CTRL+ESC: Open Start menu
- ALT+F4: Quit program
- SHIFT+DELETE: Delete item permanently
- Windows Logo + L: Lock the computer

Windows Programs Keyboard Shortcut

- CTRL+C: Copy
- CTRL+X: Cut
- CTRL+V: Paste
- CTRL+Z: Undo
- CTRL+B: Bold
- CTRL+U: Underline
- CTRL+I: Italic
- CTRL+A: Selects all the text
- CTRL+F: Find

Internet Browser Shortcuts

- CTRL+F Find
- CTRL+J: Download Folder
- CTRL+H: History Log

Windows Mouse Shortcuts

- Right Click – Shortcut menu
- Double Click – Selects a word; Launches an application
- Triple Click – Selects a paragraph
- Click followed by a SHIFT+Click – Selects text or files from the first click to the shift click
- CTRL+Click – Continues to select text or files
- SHIFT+Drag – Moves item
- CTRL+Drag – Copies the item

Glossary of Terms

 # Hashtag - Hashtags are used on social networking sites to make a word or phrase easily searchable. I have noticed it's starting to be used in everyday conversation to emphasize a word or phrase. The other day my daughter commented on something my husband and I were talking about saying "#oldpeopleproblems."

Ad network - Patty, the Millionaire Matchmaker helps people find love by pairing them with the right guy with the right girl, an ad network helps people make money by matching advertisers with publishers (bloggers.)

Add-ons/Extensions - mini applications or functions that you let you add features to your browser.

AdSense - Googles AdSense lets publishers create placeholders for ads on their website. These placeholders can be very specific about the type of ads, the placement, the size and the appearance of ads the publisher will allow to be served on their site. Google serves ads from its huge database of

AdWords customers. When someone clicks on an ad shown on a publisher site Google pays them.

AdWords - Google's AdWords makes it easy for advertisers to serve ads to their target market. When an advertiser sets up an ad they give Google a list of criteria, including keywords, for where their ad should be served.

Affiliate - in the world of online marketing an affiliate is someone who promotes a product, service or website for a commission.

Android - a mobile operating system created by Google to run portable devices like smart phones, tablets and eReaders. The versions of Android all have names of sweet food that is related to the time of year of the release, like Ice Cream Sandwich was released in the summer, Gingerbread in the winter and Jellybean in the spring.

Avatar - the little picture next to your name when you make a post on Facebook. The technical definition is a graphic representation of a person on the Internet.

Back links - any link to a site is considered a back link.

Blog - way back in time, some may call it the Stone Age of technology, people with Internet connections thought it would be neat to write about their lives and share their writings with friends and families, those writings were called web logs. Eventually the phrase web log morphed into the word blog. Unlike traditional websites blogs are meant to be interactive and to promote discussions between writers and readers. Many websites are now set up just for the purpose of blogging and most traditional websites have a blog section.

Blogging platform - you create documents in a word processor, edit photos in photo imaging software, to build a blog you use software or an application known as a blogging platform.

Brand partnership - Sally has a popular scrapbooking blog. Fiskars, a brand of scrapbooking products likes her content and think they can generate sales from her blog. Fiskars asks Sally to endorse their products in return for free products or cold hard cash. Sally and Fiskars have entered into a brand partnership, which Sally is required by the FTC to clearly state on her site.

Browser – a browser is software on your computer that allows you to visit websites and use web applications. It is like an operating system for the Internet. There are four main browsers: Google Chrome, Internet Explorer, Firefox and Safari (for the Mac). Like different word processors each browser offers different features and a different browsing experience.

Cache - Right now it is the beginning of February and I have the documents I need to do our taxes sitting in a folder on my desk. Once I'm finished with our taxes for the year I will put the file away in my closet with other important documents I need to keep but I don't need to use on a regular basis. If the tax folder is still on my desk in July and so are all the other folders I've needed since February, my desk will be cluttered, making it difficult to find what I need quickly. Cache is the place your computer puts the files it is currently using so it can find them quickly. Just like your desk needs regular cleaning so does your computer's cache.

Cloud Computing - When I worked on the help desk, sometime it was easier (or more diplomatic) to tell users their problem was caused by gremlins in the computer. Obviously there were no gremlins but they accepted this explanation and I could go about my day. I have a feeling some engineer was trying to explain files and programs being stored at a remote location and accessed through the internet to some big wig executive by saying it is in the clouds. The big wig executive took it literally and now everyone calls it cloud computing.

Content curation - you know on American Idol when they tell the contestants to take a song everyone already knows and add a new twist to it? A content curator finds the best of the best in a given topic and shares it with their opinions, comments or unique twist. If you have ever shared an article, photo or video on Facebook you have been a content curator.

Contextual advertising - the key to Google is words, actually keywords. When a blogger writes a blog post, if they had done their homework they know the right keyword phrases that will match what users are searching for and what advertisers are paying for. Google's spiders read content looking for keywords to serve relevant advertisements to the readers of the content. For example when you read my post about being a puppy parent you may see ads for dog products.

Cookie - businesses want to make your visit to their website as easy and pleasant as they can, while maximizing their profits. To accomplish some of these goals they record data about your visit and store it on your hard drive in what is called a cookie. It's like when you walk into your favorite restaurant and the bartender starts to make your favorite drink. If you clean the cookies from your hard drive the website doesn't remember you anymore, like if there is a new person behind the bar. Google also uses cookies to track your browsing history so they can serve you ads you may be interested in as you are searching and browsing the Internet.

Cropping - Just like in traditional scrapbooking cropping means to cut away the parts of an image you don't want.

Desktop - a computer, which unlike a laptop is large, made up of many components. Desktop also means the screen that is always behind all the open windows on your computer.

Direct messaging (DM) - social media networks are made up of public conversations but there are times you may want to speak privately with a friend or follower. Most sites like Facebook and Twitter have a way to do this called direct messaging. It's how you whisper virtually.

Domain Name - a domain name is an easy way to remember an internet site you like to visit. When you type www.RetiredHousewife.com in a browser's address bar the browser will go to my blog, Typing Amazon.com or Zappos.com will take you to the greatest online shopping sites ever created. For the latest gossip you can check out perezhilton.com or radaronline.com. These are all examples of domain names.

Domain Name Servers - we speak one way, the computer speaks a different way. Domain name servers are used to translate our words to numbers the computer can process. I see "retiredhousewife" and read Retired Housewife, the computer sees "retiredhousewife" and it thinks, "I don't know what that means I need to go find the numbers that are associated with those letters so I can go to that address." The numbers associated with a domain name server are known as an IP addresses.

Download - copying a file from an outside source, like the internet or a memory card, to your hard drive.

Emoticon - clever symbols created with the characters on a standard keyboard to express a mood or feeling :-}. You know those people who use hearts for dots over I they are the same people that use emoticons.

eReader - A device used to read electronic books (eBooks.) eReaders are different from tablets in that they can only be used to read eBooks. The first eReader to gain popularity was Amazon's Kindle.

Favicon - when you open a window in most browsers the browser creates a tab. These tabs allow you to have more than one site open at a time. A web master can add a tiny image to be displayed on their websites tab. These tiny images are called favicons and they are used to easily identify a site.

File Compression - it's like Spanx for computer files. Redundant information is recorded in computer shorthand, so once it is uncompressed everything goes back where it is supposed to be. Which is unlike Spanx, because when you take Spanx off everything goes back where it is not supposed to be.

Firewall - Your front door is your first level of protection against an intruder, a firewall is the computer network's first level of protection against intruders, also known as hackers who want to steal information off your computer's hard drive. Sometimes the firewall misidentifies a request to enter the network as a threat. This happened to me when I tried to set up a new blu-ray player to stream video from Netflix. My router wouldn't let it connect because it thought it was an intruder.

Flash drive - a portable storage device for files that plugs into a computer's USB port for easy access. There are some fun ones available on Amazon [affiliate link].

Following/friending/connected - your social media connections: twitter has followers, Facebook has friends or likes and LinkedIn has connections.

Forum - the coffee house of the Internet. People have conversations on a specific topic by leaving posts, which others can reply to, creating a two-way conversation with the participants in different places and participating at different times.

Google - noun: a company in California that provides search engine services; verb: to look up information on the Internet

Google+ - Google's social media network, which has gotten off to a slow start, but Google has nothing but time I wouldn't count them out yet.

Host - in the real world a host is someone who cares for your needs when you are in their company. A good host/ess will make sure all of their guest have a beverage, food and someone to talk with. In the virtual world a host is a server that takes care of your website. It makes sure users can access your site and that the site responds quickly to user request.

HotSpot - a portable device that delivers a Wi-Fi signal to one or more devices. Your smartphone probably has the capability of acting as a hotspot.

HTML - stands for hypertext markup language, a computer language that developers use to create websites. They use lots of cryptic symbols and text like <a href = “http://www.retiredhousewife.com”>which is the HTML code for a link to my website RetiredHousewife.com.

Hyperlink - usually a word or phrase written in blue with a blue underline that when clicked on takes you to another location on the web

Icon - is a small graphic that when clicked on starts a program, opens a document or does some other computer thing.

Keywords - the word someone types in a search engine box to find information on a particular topic. Publishers or content providers use these words strategically so their content will be found.

LinkedIn - a social network built for establishing and maintaining business relationships. One of the coolest things about LinkedIn is the graphic that shows you how you are connected to so many people.

Niche - when I first became involved in Internet marketing I let this word scare me into inaction. A niche is simply a topic. Think about a magazine rack, all those magazines represent niche markets, some are bigger than others, but they all have a clearly defined target audience. If you decide to start a blog you want to select a topic you are interested in, but that also has potential to make you some money, you want to select a profitable niche.

Operating system - your computer's operating system keeps everything working together by translating between the different components, the hardware (printer, monitor, mouse and keyboard) works with the software (Word, Excel, email, browser). It also translates your language (mouse clicks, keyboard entries) into computer language. The most popular operating systems are Windows and Mac OS X. Android is Google's operating system for mobile devices like tablets and smartphones No surprise Mac's mobile operating system is called iOS.

Organic Search Results – when you do a search the search engine returns a list of websites that match your criteria. These results are based solely on content as opposed to being paid for. You can save companies some money if their link comes up on both lists by clicking on the organic link.

Passive – money that comes in without you having to do anything.

Pay per click (ppc) – the publisher (blogger) gets paid when a user clicks on an advertisement being served on their website.

Pay per Impression (ppm) – advertisers pay to advertise on websites, some pay on a per impression basis which means for every thousand times their ad is shown they pay a fee.

PDF – short for portable document file, PDF's are used to share documents between people who use different software. PDFs are read by Adobe Reader which is a free download from Adobe.

Photo file type – Different file types store images differently. For instance jpegs compress files, png files maintain transparent areas, bitmap files are very small, and gifs can be animated. The most popular format is jpeg.

Pinterest - too much fun and very addictive. Pinterest lets you pin all the cool stuff you find on the Internet like cocktails, recipes, cocktails, funny quotes, cocktails, funny pet photos, cocktails, you get the idea. Check out my Pinterest boards at http://pinterest.com/retiredhousewif/.

Router - Cables in the ground, are connected to a box on the side of my house, which is connected to a router through a cable in my walls. Your connection may be a little different, but the idea is the same. The router transmits a signal it receives from this connection which is received by devices with external or built in wireless adapters.

Search engine - to find out what the new fashion trends are you may type "fashion trends" in the box of a search engine like Google. The search engine takes the keywords and goes through its index of websites to find the best matches for "fashion trends." It then presents the results to you in a list that has hyperlinks to the most relevant sites.

Search engine marketing (SEM) - where search engine optimization focuses on "organic results" the ones that show up in the left column of the search results page, search engine marketing is about the advertisements that show up at the top and the right column. These are the paid advertisers for specific keywords. You would think if you are paying you could select your spot, but that is not the case. Google has a very intricate auction system that takes place in a millisecond that determines which advertisements are shown. The more competitive the keyword the more you're going to pay for higher placement.

Search engine optimization (SEO) - websites are optimized using the keywords users would search on to find the information available on the website. The goal is to make it to the first page and ultimately the first spot of Google. How often do you look at the listings on page 98 of Google search results? (98 is the number of pages returned when I searched "what is search engine optimization?")

Smartphone - With a smartphone you can get e-mail, surf the net, play games, take photos and videos and a whole bunch of other stuff you shouldn't do while driving.

Social bookmarking - sites to store, organize and share stuff you find on the internet. The hottest right now is Pinterest, but others include StumbleUpon, Digg and Reddit.

Social Media - social media has fundamentally changed the way people communicate and interact with each other. By being able to connect through the Internet on sites like Facebook, LinkedIn and Twitter people have more interactions with each other I like to think of social media as the virtual back fence.

Spam - we all know spam is junk email, but do you know how it got its name? On some early message boards someone commented that some of the posts were like the word spam in the Monty Python spam skit. In the skit people repeating the word spam drown out all other conversations, much like junk email can make you miss an important email.

Spam filter - spam filters try to keep junk email or spam from reaching your inbox. Most of these filters do a good job but you should regularly check your spam folder to see if it blocked anything important.

Spider - crawler or bot-the program that goes out and reads web content so search engines can index them based on their content.

Streaming - Streaming is like catch and release. A large video or audio file comes through your internet connection, is held in temporary storage as you view or listen to it and then it is deleted.

Tablet - Tablets are smaller than laptops, but bigger than smartphones. Most have all the functionality of a smartphone and some of the functionality of a laptop.

Tabs - usually found at the top of the browser window, tabs keep multiple websites and apps easily accessible.

Tags - remember studying for the SATs? Well here's one for you: tag is to blog as index is to book. Bloggers use tags to identify important terms within their post.

Target market - a specific group of people content is created for. The target market for *The Retired*

Housewife's Guides for the Technically Challenged is women between 45 and 60, mid to upper income, college-educated, with grown children.

Touch screen - no more mice, no more keyboards, no more stylus, only your fingers are needed to use devices with touch screens.

Traffic - if you live in a major metropolitan area like I do you don't like traffic. In the virtual world traffic is the number of people who visit your site and potentially click on links which puts money in your account. Traffic is good.

Tumblr - a microblogging site that usually has a lot of photos and/or videos.

Tweet - a post of 140 characters or less that is broadcast on the social networking site Twitter.

Twitter - a microblogging site that lets people share their interests, thoughts and knowledge in 140 characters or less.

Uniform resource locator (URL)- the address of a website, mine is http://www.RetiredHousewife.com.

Upload - copying a file from your computer to an outside source. If you've ever shared a photo on Facebook you have uploaded a file. Good Job!

USB port - a place on your computer that allows you to connect devices like webcams, digital cameras and other cool stuff.

Virtual - not real, like many "friendships" on Facebook.

Vlogging - a video blog (see definition for a blog.)

Web 2.0 - until recently media (newspaper, radio, television) has been a one-way conversation. We read, listened and watched and very rarely had an opportunity to comment or engage with the author. Web 2.0 allows for and even encourages conversations between two or more people.

Wi-Fi - To connect to the internet you either need to be plugged into a router, a network or have a wireless adapter that can accept signals transmitted by a router. Public Wi-Fi signals are available at most Starbucks and Panera's.

Wireless - most keyboards and mice are wireless now, meaning they don't have a cord connecting them to the computer. They work much the same way as a TV remote control.

Zipped files - have you ever tried those space bags? You use your vacuum cleaner to suck out all the air and the bag becomes much smaller. A zipped file is like a file that has had the air sucked out of it. When you unzip the file everything goes back to the way it was much like when you let the air back into a space bag.

About the Retired Housewife

I have been married for 24 years. For most of those years I assumed the responsibilities of cleaning the house, doing the shopping, cooking meals, driving kids around, whatever needed doing, I did. I am very lucky to have a husband who is very helpful around the house, but at the end of the day it was up to me.

Three years ago, my oldest child went off to college and my husband took a new job that required him to travel. My son and I were on our own for dinner a lot. I never really liked cooking and my son didn't really like eating, well at least not a big sit down meal in the evening. He preferred Chipotle after school and a bowl of cereal before going to bed; worked for me.

I fell into a habit of not thinking about dinner. Unfortunately when my husband was home he had not fallen into the habit of not wanting to eat dinner.

He would call on his way home from work and the conversation would go something like this:

Matt: What's for dinner?

Me: Ummmm, not sure.

Matt: "I'll stop at the grocery store and get something to make."

Me: "Great."

Eventually I realized I had no intention of ever cooking dinner again. I shared this news with my husband, who kinda laughed, looked at me and said, "You're serious." And Yes I was.

It was around this time I became a Territory Owner for a company called RelyLocal. RelyLocal is a local's only online business directory. As an owner I was responsible for selling the service to local businesses, creating the listing with search engine optimization in mind and then promoting the business through online marketing. Confused? Yea so was I.

With my previous experiences as a software trainer, a help desk support analyst and technical writer I figured it would take a month or two to get up to speed on what I needed to be successful with RelyLocal. I greatly underestimated what I had missed in the last 20 or so years. Still I love learning technology and my kids were older and I wasn't cooking dinner, so I had the time to learn. I spent hours on the computer getting caught up with all the latest and greatest.

I discovered a whole new world on the internet and gave up on RelyLocal to start a blog. BlogByB. B is a nickname my daughter and her friends gave me when they were in middle school. Now my son and his friends also call me B. It was cute and catchy and my cousin made me a cute bee logo.

I created a website for my blog using WordPress. Once the site was up I learned about Google's AdSense and search engine optimization. I researched keywords, wrote blog posts, redesigned my website and did online marketing (I was on Facebook a lot). Traffic came slowly but I started making a little money.

I would emerge from my office look around and think someone should clean this place up. Then I would remember that someone was me who was supposed to clean this place up. That is when I hired the cleaning company. I think my husband was relieved. He was not used to coming home to a, not necessarily dirty house, but one that wasn't as clean or as tidy as he was used to.

One night while we were out to dinner with another couple I mentioned I don't cook dinner anymore. Later in the conversation I said something about the cleaning company who cleans our house every 2 weeks. My friend's husband looked at me and asked, "What do you do?" Huh, I had no idea how to explain it to him. I had tried explaining blogging and affiliate marketing to my friends, whose eyes would glaze over as they said, "Oh, Becky you know I'm technically challenged."

I started BlogByB with the idea that it was the anti-mommy blog. My target market wasn't a Mommy anymore (unless her kids wanted something). She was between the ages of 40 and 60, with older kids who were either on their own, in college or close to it. Originally I was thinking the blog would have fashion advice (my friends are laughing out loud right now), articles about dealing with older parents (stop laughing), my experience as a puppy parent, some technology stuff, plus things I thought were funny. I was all over the place and the exact opposite of what is called a niche.

I had always wanted part of BlogByB to be technical how-tos and tips for women. I shied away from it because I was afraid my target market wasn't interested. I know my target audience is not technically challenged they are just part of the generation that is too young to ignore technology, but too old to have grown up with it. They feel stupid asking questions and don't want to admit they don't understand the answers half of the time.

Having just taught myself all of this stuff, I know there are not a lot of resources that speak the same language as me and my friends. That is not to say therc arc not good online courses and information. It is to say that most of them are written by 20 something year old men, who started internet marketing when they were 12. They just don't speak the same language as we do when it comes to this stuff. My target market wants to learn what they need to know to get along in an increasingly technical world, but they didn't want to spend their time sitting in a classroom feeling stupid.

As I started telling people I wanted part of my blog to be about helping women understand technology. I started getting asked questions. I answered the questions in ways women understood, without all the jargon and without making them feel stupid. I figuratively (I hate when people say literally when it really isn't) saw light bulbs going off over their heads. Through short videos posted on Facebook , an occasional newsletter, online courses (coming soon), eBooks (like this one) and presentations (with or without cocktails) women are beginning to realize this technology stuff is not that difficult, when it is explained by someone who speaks the same language.

I love my little B logo and the name BlogByB, but I needed something that better explained my new focus. I am a big fan of the Bravo franchise The Real Housewives' and have actually written some blog posts title "The Real Housewives of Olney." I was trying to think of something to follow Real Housewives when I remembered the conversation I had with my friend's husband and realized I am not even a housewife anymore. In fact I am a Retired Housewife and so are most of my friends. I mean we will always be moms, some of us wives there will always be stuff to do in the house, but as kids get older and husbands get trained our "housewife" duties diminish.

These books are written for the beginner or as so many women describe themselves, technically challenged. I explain everything. Please don't think I'm insulting your intelligence, I'm not, I'm just assuming nothing. And while these guides are written with a female audience in mind, some men may pick up a thing or two.

I hope you enjoy this book and you look for future titles in the series.

Index

H

I

J

K

M

P

R

S

Made in the USA
Monee, IL
08 November 2026

67950733R00092